The Four Most Baffling Challenges for Teachers And How To Solve Them

Classroom Discipline–Unmotivated Students– Underinvolved or Adversarial Parents– And Tough Working Conditions

Sheryn Spencer Waterman

EYE ON EDUCATION

EYE ON EDUCATION
6 DEPOT WAY WEST, SUITE 106
LARCHMONT, NY 10538
(914) 833–0551
(914) 833–0761 fax
www.eyeoneducation.com

Library of Congress Cataloging-in-Publication Data

Waterman, Sheryn Spencer. The four most baffling challenges for teachers and how to solve them: classroom discipline, unmotivated students, underinvolved or adversarial parents, and tough working conditions / Sheryn Northey Waterman.
      p. cm.
Includes bibliographical references.
ISBN 1-59667-019-3
      1. Effective teaching. 2. Classroom management. 3. Motivation in education. I. Title.
LB1025.3.W38 2006
371.1—dc22

                                                        2005034893

10 9 8 7 6 5 4 3 2 1

Editorial and production services provided by
Richard H. Adin Freelance Editorial Services
52 Oakwood Blvd., Poughkeepsie, NY 12603-4112
(845-471-3566)

Also Available from EYE ON EDUCATION

**Handbook on Differentiated Instruction
For Middle and High Schools**
Sheryn Spencer Waterman

**What Great Teachers Do Differently:
14 Things That Matter Most**
Todd Whitaker

**Classroom Motivation From A to Z:
How to Engage Your Students in Learning**
Barbara R. Blackburn

**BRAVO Teacher!
Building Relationships with Actions That Value Others**
Sandra Harris

Great Quotes for Great Educators
Todd Whitaker and Dale Lumpa

**What Great Principals Do Differently:
15 Things That Matter Most**
Todd Whitaker

**101 "Answers" for New Teachers and Their Mentors:
Effective Teaching Tips for Daily Classroom Use**
Annette L. Breaux

**Talk It Out!
The Educator's Guide to Successful Difficult Conversations**
Barbara E. Sanderson

**Differentiated Instruction:
A Guide for Elementary School Teachers**
Amy Benjamin

**What Successful Principals Do!
169 Tips for Principals**
Franzy Fleck

**Motivating & Inspiring Teachers:
The Educational Leader's Guide for Building Staff Morale**
Todd Whitaker, Beth Whitaker, and Dale Lumpa

Table of Contents

1

The Four Most Baffling Challenges for Teachers

This book is about dealing with the four most common challenges for teachers. As you will see, there is a great deal of information about how to deal with these four challenges:

◆ Discipline

◆ Unmotivated students

◆ Underinvolved or adversarial parents

◆ Tough working conditions

In my years of teaching, I have dealt with various aspects of each of these challenges. Sometimes solutions were simple, but often solutions tested my character and skills. Fortunately, my struggles with these challenges have led to my growth as a professional teacher and as a person. When I started this book, I made a commitment to learn as much as I could about these challenges so that I could provide the information to my colleagues as a kind of executive summary of what is out there. Because this is the information age, information is easy to get; however, there is too much of it and new ideas pop up daily. I have read extensively on these topics, and I present an overview of research and resources that address each one. I also offer a criterion for judging the solutions I found in my reading and in my experience. I also offer a suggestion for decision making based on a synthesis of the information and my experiences as a classroom teacher. I give examples of how I solved issues related to these challenges. Although these examples are based on real events, they have been fictionalized to protect those involved from being identified.

I hope this book provides some possible solutions that could help make teaching more rewarding and that it might even prevent good teachers from leaving the classroom. If you are affected by any of these challenges, or if you know someone who is, please check out this book. Read it chapter by chapter or just read the chapters that address your particular challenges.

How to Evaluate Solutions

In addition to these challenges, there is another underlying challenge: deciding what solutions to choose. Making decisions about how to deal with these challenges can feel like a tug of war; each side of the issue has undeniable, empirical evidence through research that their ideas are superior to the other side's ideas. Therefore, a significant challenge for you is to decide which solutions are right for you, your students, and your school.

Many departments of instruction insist that any program or strategy adopted by a school system be *research based;* however, it may be wise to use not only the evidence of research, but also to use other criteria. As you consider how to deal effectively with challenges in your classroom, school, or district, the first thing you might do is think about various responses in terms of your own belief system. You may discover that many solutions to challenges in the classroom are counterintuitive (i.e., seem to go against reason). Ways to deal with challenges may seem counterintuitive because your belief system could be tied to theories and concepts that have been replaced by ideas that in close analysis make more sense for today's children, young people, and adults.

Todd Whitaker, author of the inspirational book, *What Great Teachers Do Differently: 14 Things that Matter Most* (2004), says that it is people, not programs, that make excellent teachers and excellent schools; however, it is beneficial to establish a basic criterion that might help teachers decide what solutions to choose. This criterion can help teachers answer the questions they should ask when they make decisions about dealing with challenges: Does this solution add value to the people involved? And does it resolve the situation/challenge effectively? For example, if I use a discipline method that helps my students learn better self-control and helps me learn to be more skilled at being kind while firm, then that discipline method added value to the situation. However, if I use a discipline method that makes a student angry and embarrassed and puts me in the role of enemy rather than helper, then that method has not added value; it has hurt both the student and me.

The BESST Criterion

What follows is an explanation and examples of a criterion that adds value to the lives of those involved in schools. As you will see, I summarize and draw conclusions about some important ideas I believe will be most helpful to you as you deal with these four challenges and others.

This criterion is based on relatively new education concepts: brain-based research, levels of ethical development, the standards movement, and systems theory. Basing a criterion on these four ideas seems to have the most to offer for these reasons:

♦ These are relatively new ideas whose purpose is to improve education. For instance, some of this information was not available to many teachers before the 1990s. Now that it is available, we can use it to help with these challenges.

♦ Using four ideas instead of one, gives a broader base to decision making.

I propose a criterion that summarizes and simplifies these concepts in order to make them useful for teachers and that add value to the lives of those involved. I do not like using acronyms for programs; however, when you are learning something, an acronym can help you remember until you incorporate the information into our way of being. Therefore, I have chosen an acronym for my criterion and present it as a simple formula: the BESST (brain-based, ethical, standards-based, systems theory) Criterion = Value Added.

In the following pages, I provide summaries of information about the four areas that make up the criterion, and then I present a synthesis of that information in a chart that might help you evaluate solutions to your challenges. In the chapters that follow, I include a thorough discussion of each of the four challenges and show you how to use the chart to evaluate solutions to these challenges. I also describe a model of decision-making that incorporates the BESST Criterion and show you how to use it in real situations. And finally, I propose criteria for a caring-based education organization.

Brain-Based Research

Brain-based research has unlocked many of the secrets that limited scientific capability denied us for many years. Although we do not know everything about how the brain functions, we know a great deal more now than did scientists like B. F. Skinner and Abraham Maslow (1962) when they were developing theories about learning. Many of the findings of brain-based research support what researchers in the past could only assume from their subjects' behaviors; however, some of the original findings are not supported by this newer research. Unfortunately, old ideas die hard, and even though some ideas have been disproved, people still hold on to them as if they were true. Brain-based researcher Eric Jensen explains in his book *Teaching With the Brain in Mind* (1998) that we now have evidence that disputes certain commonly held ideas about leaning. One of the most important findings is the idea that the brain has its own reward system.

Knowing that many teachers rely heavily on rewarding students as a way to motivate them, Jensen suggests that instead of asking what they can do to motivate students, he says a better question to ask is, what is going on in the brain when students are motivated? His ideas (p. 68) are illustrated in the accompanying image, "Practical Alternatives to Using Rewards." Jensen warns that if teachers withdraw rewards, students may initially seem to do poorly; however, for the sake of students' well-being, teachers should not give up finding ways to naturally engage the desire to learn.

Practical Alternatives to Using Rewards

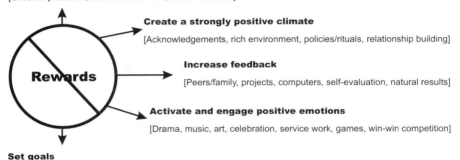

Eliminate threat
[Uncover problems, add transition time, avoid demands]

Create a strongly positive climate
[Acknowledgements, rich environment, policies/rituals, relationship building]

Increase feedback
[Peers/family, projects, computers, self-evaluation, natural results]

Activate and engage positive emotions
[Drama, music, art, celebration, service work, games, win-win competition]

Set goals
[Meaning making, student choices, valid reasons, clear purpose]

Example: Some programs align themselves with brain-based research and some do not. Though you may believe what the brain-based researchers are saying, it may not fit well with your own situation. For instance, a middle school team of highly capable teachers was having so much trouble with their students that they were willing to try anything to get them under control. Even though some of them believed that bribing students to behave was counterproductive, they needed something. They brought out a competition, which went like this: Students who behaved exceptionally well in class received a ticket that they could place in a pot. At the end of the month, someone would draw names out of the pot for various prizes, the grand prize being the whole pot.

Did it work? Some teachers felt they had to participate because they did not want to go against the team's wishes; however, they did not actually give out tickets and none of their students asked for them. On occasion, they found tickets on the floor that students had dropped. They had the drawing, some students won, but students' behavior was still bad. Teachers put a great deal of time and their own money into this reward system for very little, if any, change in their situation.

Teachers should carefully consider the key elements of brain-based research as relevant criteria by which to judge the solutions to the challenges. These elements can be summarized as follows: *In an environment where stu-*

dents' goals are aligned with classroom experiences, the brain motivates itself to learn without being bribed by rewards or threatened with punishment.

Ethics

The highest level of ethical behavior is not determined by the prevailing rules of society or from the dictates of government. It comes from a deep sense of love. Many religions provide the basis for this love, for instance Judeo-Christian and Eastern religions (Confucianism, Taoism, and Hinduism) share a belief in the benefits of doing to others as you would have them do to you (the Golden Rule) and never intentionally harming anyone. Without the religious element, these beliefs are called secular humanism, but both religious-based and nonreligious-based values that show love and caring for others are humanistic. I propose that all teacher decisions be based on humanistic and ethical values and that they are *caring-based*.

I have included ethics as part of the criterion because I believe that although most people, especially teachers, want to behave based on highest ethics, the desire does not always match the implementation. Measuring a program against the standards of kindness, respect, and mutuality, has to be an important criterion for judging a solution to a challenge.

Example: Many school systems clearly value ethical behavior from teachers and administrators, especially when it comes to "testing ethics." However, I cannot give examples of ongoing discussions among teachers in terms of the ethics involved in their decision making. We seem to leave this issue out when we are discussing interventions with students. I hope this book will inspire such discussions. To summarize: *Teachers should consider that all people (including children) are created equal with equal rights to freedom, happiness, and the Golden Rule (being treated as you would like to be treated).*

Standards

Most people recognize that someone who is chosen Teacher of the Year or for other teaching awards is probably a good teacher, but before the 1990s there was no unified consensus as to what defines a great teacher or a great school. In the 1990s, the standards movement began when three major organizations were formed: The National Board for Professional Teaching Standards (NBPTS), the Interstate New Teachers Assessment and Support Consortium (INTASC), and the National Council for Teaching and America's Future (NCTAF). From these collaborative organizations, came researched-based and thoroughly debated lists of standards and suggestions.

The standards movement offers us some useful ideas about how to deal with these challenges based on the judgments of well-informed and committed education stakeholders. "Comparison of Credential Standards" is a chart showing the standards from three leading credentialing organizations: the

National Board for Professional Teaching Standards (NBPTS), the National Council for the Accreditation of Teacher Education (NCATE), and the Southern Association of Colleges and Schools Council on Accreditation and School Improvement (SACSCASI). The Southern Association of Colleges and Schools is a regional organization, and I presume each region of the United States has a similar organization. The chart shows standards from each of these organizations in terms of the four challenges.

Looking at the standards given here in this comparative chart, one can see patterns that support the following ideas:

♦ All students can learn.

♦ Educators should understand the context (system) in which they interact with students.

♦ All stakeholders should collaborate to determine important school decisions.

♦ Disciplinary actions should preserve dignity and promote citizenship.

♦ Educators should be partners with parents who participate in school decision making.

♦ Working conditions should be safe and conducive to learning.

♦ Teachers, administrators, and the school should understand how students are motivated to learn.

♦ Educators should be sensitive to issues of diversity.

♦ Educators should have extensive knowledge and skills in their area of work within the school.

♦ Educators should be human development experts.

Example: No other programs in education have matched the impact the of National Board certification on teaching in my state. The work teachers do to obtain National Board certification exemplifies the best in professional development practices. Research has shown that National Board Certified teachers outperform those who are not National Board Certified on 11 out of 13 indicators related to student achievement (Bond, Smith, Baker, & Hattie, 2000). In addition to this research, there several other studies have been completed, or are ongoing, that show excellent correlation between the National Board process and many issues that affect schools. If you are interested in examining all or some of these studies, you might go the National Board website (www.NBPTS.org) and click on the "Research" section. The standards movement in the case of improving teaching is well documented.

Comparison of Credential Standards

Categories	NBPTS (Master teacher standards)[1]	SACSCASI (School standards)[2]	NCATE (Standards for organizations that prepare teachers for P12 schools)[3]
Discipline	Accomplished teachers know how to engage groups of students to ensure a disciplined learning environment.Equally important (to cognition), they foster students' self-esteem, motivation, character, civic responsibility, and their respect for individual, cultural, religious and racial differences.Teachers are responsible for managing and monitoring student learning....	The school fosters and maintains a safe and orderly environment that promotes honesty, integrity, trustworthiness, responsibility, citizenship, self-discipline, and respect; provides students opportunities to develop and demonstrate leadership, responsibility, independence, and decision-making skills,. . . monitors students attendance and conduct.	Teacher candidates...have a positive effect on all students. They create an environment conducive to learning.
Student Motivation	Accomplished teachers...treat students equitably, recognizing the individual differences that distinguish one student from another and taking account of these differences in their practice. They adjust their practice based on observation and knowledge of their students' interests abilities, skills, knowledge, family...circumstances and peer relationships. Accomplished teachers understand how students develop and learn. They incorporate the prevailing theories of cognition and intelligence in their practice. They are aware of the influence of context [i.e. systems] and culture on behavior. Accomplished teachers know how to motivate students to learn and how to maintain their interest in the face of temporary failure. Accomplished teachers create enrich, maintain and alter instruction settings to capture and sustain the interest of their students and to make the most effect use of time.	The school offers curriculum that challenges each student to excel and that reflects a commitment to equity, an appreciation for diversity, and a recognition of different ways of learning;...accommodates diverse learning styles; promotes the active involvement of students in the learning process...and that they may apply their skills and their learning in diverse ways.	Teacher candidates reflect on their practice and make necessary adjustments to enhance student learning. They know how students learn and how to make ideas accessible to them. Teacher candidates are able to create learning environments encouraging positive social interaction, active engagement in learning and self-motivation. They foster active inquiry, collaboration, and support interaction in the classroom. They evaluate students' academic achievement as well as their social and physical development with the results to maximize students' motivation and learning. Teacher candidates know the ways children and adolescents learn and develop, including the cognitive and affective development and the relationship of these to learning.

Categories	NBPTS (Master teacher standards)[1]	SACSCASI (School standards)[2]	NCATE (Standards for organizations that prepare teachers for P12 schools)[3]
Parents	Accomplished teachers find ways to work collaboratively and creatively with parents, engaging them productively the work of the school. Accomplished teachers…can clearly explain student performance to parents. Frequent and thorough two-way communication with parents.	The school fosters partnerships through collaboration with community stakeholders to support student learning, ensures clear and effective communications among and between all stakeholders, solicits the knowledge and skills of parents to enhance the work of the school, communicates to all stakeholders the expectations for student learning and the results of school improvement efforts.	Teacher candidates consider…family and community contexts in connecting concepts to students' prior experiences and applying the ideas to real-world problems. Candidates work with students, families, and communities in ways that reflect the dispositions expected of professional educators.
Working Conditions	Teachers are members of learning communities: Accomplished teachers contribute to the effectiveness of the school by working collaboratively with other professionals on instructional policy, curriculum development, and staff development.	The school ensures that professional staff collaboratively gathers data…[and] sustains a climate that is conducive to teaching and learning. The school provides facilities, equipment, and a site necessary for effective implementation of the instructional and extracurricular programs; possesses and implements a plan for maintaining and improving the site, facilities and equipment; maintains the site, facilities, and equipment to provide an environment that is healthy and safe for all occupants. The school monitors school climate and takes appropriate steps to ensure that it is conducive to student learning.	All school personnel are expected to carry out their work in ways supportive of student learning. Teacher candidates continually reflect on their choices and actions on others and actively seek opportunities to grow professionally. They also are able to foster relationships with colleagues….

1. Online at www.nbpts.org.
2. Online at www.Sacscasi.org.
3. Online at www.ncate.org/public/standards.asp.

Other Views of Excellent Teachers

In addition to standards developed by diverse groups, we also have the wisdom of exceptional individual educators who from their own experience define great teachers. Here is an overview of Todd Whitaker's ideas about what great teachers do, and a quote from Deborah Meier about the qualities a teacher should have.

Todd Whitaker's View

In *What Great Teachers Do Differently: 14 Things that Matter Most* (2004), Todd Whitaker suggests the following (pp. 127–128):

1. Great teachers never forget that it is people, not programs, that determine the quality of a school.
2. Great teachers establish clear expectations at the start of the year and follow them consistently as the year progresses.
3. When a student misbehaves, great teachers have one goal, to keep that behavior from happening again.
4. Great teachers have high expectations for students but even higher expectations for themselves.
5. Great teachers know who is the variable in the classroom. *They are!* Good teachers consistently strive to improve, and they focus on something they can control-their own performance.
6. Great teachers create a positive atmosphere in their classrooms and schools. They treat every person with respect. In particular, they understand the power of praise.
7. Great teachers consistently filter out the negatives that don't matter and share a positive attitude.
8. Great teachers work hard to keep their relationships in good repair-to avoid personal hurt and to repair any possible damage.
9. Great teachers have the ability to ignore trivial disturbances and the ability to respond to inappropriate behavior without escalating the situation.
10. Great teachers have a plan and purpose for everything they do. If things don't work out the way they had envisioned, they reflect on what they could have done differently and adjust their plans accordingly.
11. Before making any decision or attempting to bring about any change, great teachers ask themselves one central question: *What will the best people think?*

12. Great teachers continually ask themselves who is most comfortable and who is least comfortable with each decision they make. They treat everyone as if they were good.

13. Great teachers keep standardized testing in perspective; they center on the real issue of student learning.

14. Great teachers care about their students. They understand that behaviors and beliefs are tied to emotion, and they understand the power of emotion to jump-start change.

Deborah Meier's view

Deborah Meier, in her book *The Power of Their Ideas* (1995, 2002), lists these five qualities to look for in a teacher (p. 142):

◆ A self-conscious reflectiveness about how they themselves learn and (maybe even more important) about how and when they *don't* learn

◆ A sympathy toward others, an appreciation of differences, an ability to imagine one's own "otherness"

◆ A willingness, better yet a taste, for working collaboratively

◆ A passion for having others share some of one's own interests

◆ A lot of perseverance, energy, and devotion to getting things right

To summarize: *Highly qualified educators should have extensive skills and knowledge in order to provide a positive learning environment in close collaboration with all stakeholders.*

Systems Theory

Systems theory is a relatively recent conceptual framework, but teachers use *systems thinking* all the time. For instance, when you analyze your seating arrangement to determine how various students' behaviors interact with other students' behaviors, you are using systems thinking. When you determine that a student needs some extra attention because you know his parents are divorcing, you are thinking systemically.

Systems thinking is about looking at the big picture and noticing the relationships within that picture. When systems thinkers plan their actions or react to behaviors, they consider the impact of their actions on not only parts of the system (i.e., the individual), but also they consider the impact on the whole system. For instance, Todd Whitaker suggests a systemic-like intervention that includes having "25 students on the teacher's side." He says that when one student misbehaves, the whole class (all 26 students) is affected, and they count on the teacher to deal with that misbehavior fairly. If the class believes the teacher's actions are overly punitive and unfair, most likely the whole class will turn against that teacher making it nearly impossible for him to teach.

Example: An example of the importance of using systems thinking in all aspects of teaching comes from my experience as an academic facilitator. I had to enter other teachers' classrooms, respect their authority, and present myself as a peer even though I was demonstrating a lesson idea they were learning from me. One of the highlights of my career came when I demonstrated a Hilda Taba concept development strategy in a teacher's room. I had no idea if she would use the strategy or not. Sometimes I would demonstrate a lesson and a teacher would use that time to grade papers and take a break. It was totally up to the teacher to use the demonstrated strategy. In this case, I was delighted to see that this teacher not only used the strategy, but she found an even better way to implement it. If I had not known how to enter a system (her classroom) respectfully, I may not have had any impact at all.

Although systemic thinking might be new to you, I hope you will give it a chance. I explain more about systems theory in the following chapters; however, if I do not explain it well enough for your needs, you might read some of Peter Senge's books, *Schools that Learn* (2000) and/or *The Fifth Discipline* to get a more thorough understanding of this useful way of thinking about teaching and learning. To summarize: *Having an awareness of the interactions that make up an environment helps teachers respectfully and strategically plan their actions.*

The BESST Criterion = Value Added

Now that I have explained these four concepts, I have condensed them into a chart that may help you evaluate the various solutions and ideas I present in the remainder of this book. I show you how to use the criterion so that using it equals added value to the solution or situation; however, I would encourage you to use it from your own perspective in order to evaluate the various solutions to your challenges.

How to Use the Chart

As you consider solutins to your challenges, read the chart, but do not limit yourself to my summaries. Think about what you know about brain-based research, ethics, standards, and systems. Compare a solution strategy to what you know about these four areas and check off in your mind or physically put a check or plus by each of the criteria that is aligned with a solution or philosophy. Think about how the strategy or philosophy may not be aligned with this criterion and cross off in your mind or actually put an X or negative by each of the criteria that is not present in a solution or philosophy.

BESST Criterion = Value Added

Brain-Based	Ethical	Standards	Systems Theory
In an environment where students' goals are aligned with classroom experiences, the brain motivates itself to learn without being bribed by rewards or threatened by punishment.	All people (including children) are created equal with equal rights to freedom, happiness, and the Golden Rule.	Extensive skills and knowledge help teachers provide a positive learning environment.	Having an awareness of the interactions that make up an environment helps teachers respectfully and strategically plan their actions.

Applying the Chart to a Specific Issue

What follows is a discussion of two opposing perspectives that overarch the four challenges. I will discuss these opposing views in terms of the BESST Criteria = Value Added; however, I would encourage you to evaluate them from your own perspective as well.

How Do You View Relationships?

Do you see relationships with others in terms of power-over hierarchy (one person or entity has *power over* another or a group)? Or do you see relationships with others as collaborative, where people work for the *mutual* benefit of all involved, and where their roles are different in function but equal in respect and status? See how these views are described in the accompanying chart ("Relationship Views").

Relationship Views

Collaboration	Power-Over Hierarchy
One person or persons must join with others to mutually address everyone's needs in order to deal with a challenge.	One person or persons must have power over others in order to deal with most challenges. For instance, when it comes to making tough decisions, one person or group needs to be in charge.
Leadership is collaborative.	Leadership is top-down.
Organizing concept is mutuality.	Organizing concept is power-over.

Which View Do You Take?

Is your belief system on the left or on the right of the "Relationship Views" chart? Also, more importantly, do your actions align with your view? As you analyze these opposing views, based on your own belief system and the BESST Criterion, did you choose a side or end up somewhere in the middle. What is your *truth* about relationships?

My View

As I analyze these two sides, I would say that collaboration is superior to power-over hierarchy in terms of the BESST Criteria for the following reasons:

♦ Brain-based: Collaboration creates an environment where *goals are aligned* with experiences because all members of the environment have a say in how the goals are determined; therefore, the brain will *motivate itself without being bribed by rewards or threatened with punishment. All will have ownership of those goals, and will work to accomplish them.* Even if the results are not perfect, at least everyone knows they were responsible and can feel positive about taking action based on their own volition. Power-over hierarchy counts on one person or persons being able to determine what goals would be best for others. This is unrealistic, even though it may seem to work, because powerful people or people in powerful positions can manipulate or intimidate others into agreeing with them. Only through defiance or compliance will the goals be addressed, with mixed results.

♦ Ethics: Collaboration supports the idea that *all people (including children) are created equal with equal rights to freedom, happiness, and the Golden Rule (being treated as you would like to be treated)* because collaboration is doing something together for the benefit of all involved. Power-over hierarchy does not support equality because it assumes certain people are more capable than others and should exert power over others whether they need that power or not. If power is used to nurture and support, it must be used with a sense of equality, which is not reflected in paternalistic, top-down hierarchies.

◆ Standards: All of the standards support collaboration. They state that a *positive learning environment* should occur in close collaboration with all involved. For instance, the standards say all stakeholders should be closely involved with school-based decision making. The standards assume that *all stakeholders have skills and knowledge* and should be viewed as valuable for every aspect of decision making.

◆ Systems Theory: Collaboration is supported by systems thinking because it is respectful of the *interactions within an environment and it suggests teachers plan action based on that respect.* In power-over hierarchy, asking for change can be a disrespectful process because one person or group may be using personal power to tell people what to do. They may also abuse the power that has been assigned to their position rather than having a true respect and concern for the interactions among others within the system.

◆ = Added Value? When using collaboration you will add value to the lives of those involved because learning to get along with others in order to collaborate is a highly valued skill. For instance, the ability to negotiate, to use personal power to support and nurture, and to resolve situations in a win-win manner have become the more valued ways of dealing with issues, solving problems, and dealing with challenges. Although many people still believe it is quicker and sometimes easier to use power-over decision making, they would admit that reaching consensus and developing ownership among all involved gets more valuable long-term results.

How Will You Use This Information to Deal With the Challenges?

Your knowledge of the theories and practices presented in this book may influence you to choose to make major changes in your classroom. You may even feel compelled to push for change in your school, district, state, or nation when you think about how a variety of issues can work against your ability to deal effectively with the students in your care. Even if you know what you need to do for your students, you may be working in a system that prevents you from implementing your ideas.

Choosing How to Deal With the Four Challenges: Three Ideas

I would encourage you to evaluate all theories or practices that seem to resonate with your belief system; and based on the BESST Criterion = Value Added formula. If you cannot honestly say that the model or program adds value to the lives of your students, to the adults with whom you work, and to yourself, then you might not want to use it. The ideas are laid out in "Three Ideas for Four Challenges."

Three Ideas for Four Challenges

Idea #1: *Implement specific models or suggestions.*
Take the following steps: • Choose a specific model(s) or suggestion to deal with the challenge or challenges you face. • Learn as much as you can about that model. • Get training if necessary. • Find someone who knows how to implement the model or suggestion to coach you as you practice the strategies of that model or suggestion. • Make the model your own, but do not vary too much from the ideas developed by the author. (Nothing ruins a great concept like poor implementation.) • If your challenges go beyond your own classroom, collaborate and provide leadership to implement the model(s) or suggestion(s) you believe will deal most effectively with the challenges in your school, district, state, or nation.
Idea #2: *Notice patterns from many sources and develop your own solutions.*
Take the following steps: • Read several suggestions that deal with your specific challenge or challenges. • Decide which ideas resonate with your views. • Notice patterns in how others deal with specific challenges. • Use your understanding of those patterns to design your own plan of implementation. • Collaborate with others who share your views. • Provide leadership to implement your ideas in your own classroom, school, district, state, or nation.
Idea #3: *Use the Five Pause-Point system of decision making based on BESST Criterion.*
I suggest using the Five Pause-Point system of decision making to create any strategy that you might use in the classroom, with a parent, or with an administrator. For the classroom, I suggest it as an alternative to models that focus only on student achievement. Perhaps these ideas could be used in conjunction with data analysis to remind you that you *are* dealing

with a human being, not a number or set of numbers. With parents, it should help you stay on their side for the well-being of their child. It should help you avoid adversarial relationships and promote partnership. With administrators, it should help you promote collaboration and partnership rather than adversarial, abusive exchanges.

This decision-making model functions in a spiraling manner, as depicted in the accompanying figure, "Five Pause-Point Decision-Making Model." It begins with you needing to choose an action. It may be an action that can be thoroughly planned, or it may be a split-second action that you must take when confronted with a problem or an issue. I call these *pause-points* because sometimes they are actually deliberate steps we take, but other times they are truly ongoing and overlapping, so that they are not actually distinct steps.

These points are artificial pauses in an ongoing overlapping process. With these pauses, we can simulate the process of freezing time or slowing it down so that we can say to ourselves, "What am I actually thinking or doing in this moment?" If you could freeze time, you might find yourself asking questions that keep you honest with yourself and require you to reflect on a deep level about a planned or unplanned action. Remembering that inaction is also an action, you should proceed in a spiraling manner as follows:

Pause 1—Planning: First, when you need to plan a lesson, respond to a student's behavior, deal with a parent, or collaborate with an administrator, you should think of the answers to questions like these:

1. Will my action be in line with brain-based research? For instance, will I avoid bribery or punishment and will my goals be aligned with students' goals?

2. Will my action be ethical? Will it hurt anyone (including myself) or help anyone (including myself)?

3. Will my action reflect the standards? For instance, will it demonstrate skill and knowledge to create a positive atmosphere?

4. Will my action be sensitive to the systems I will affect?

5. What will I do? Sometimes you may not have the answers quickly; therefore, you might take some time to think about your answers. Other times you may not have the luxury of taking some time to think, but *some* time is better than an impetuous action.

Pause 2: Implementation and Observation: The next step in the process is implementing the action. This action could be a lesson, a disciplinary procedure, or a conference with a parent or administrator. As you are implementing the action, observe closely the reaction of the person or persons who have been the recipients of the action. If you can take notes on your observations, you will have even better information because it can be hard to remember everything in order to participate in the next step.

Pause 3—Reflection: Following this keen observation, you should then reflect about what you observed from the parent, students, or administrator, and then ask yourself the same questions you asked in the planning phase:

1. Is my action in line with brain-based research? For instance, did I avoid bribery or punishment and were my goals aligned with students' goals?

2. Is my action ethical? Did it hurt anyone (including myself) or help anyone (including myself)?

3. Does my action reflect the standards? For instance, did it demonstrate skill and knowledge to create a positive atmosphere?

4. Is my action sensitive to the systems I will affect?

5. What will I do?

Pause 4—Revision: Based on the answers to these questions, you might choose to revise your actions to make them more closely aligned with the BESST Criterion. You might change your lesson to make it useful to more students; apologize to a parent or student because on closer evaluation, you made a mistake; or ask for another chance to deal with an issue.

Pause 5—Acting with More Knowledge—Adding Value: As you make more decisions about how to act; you are even more knowledgeable about your choices and the effects of your decisions. You can continue to plan and act with your students', your own, and others' best interests in mind. You have added value to your life and the lives of those you teach.

Five Pause-Point Decision-Making Model

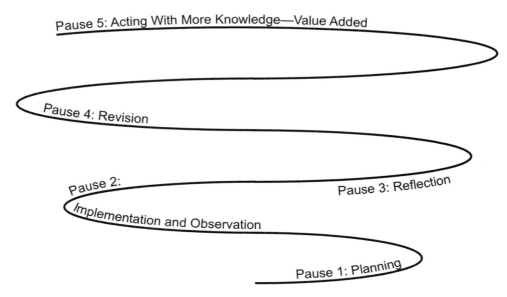

Pause 5: Acting With More Knowledge—Value Added

Pause 4: Revision

Pause 2: Implementation and Observation

Pause 3: Reflection

Pause 1: Planning

To help you apply the Five Pause-Point Model to the four challenges, I provide a real-life example using this model in each chapter.

Summary

I have provided you with ways to make your own choices about how to deal with the four challenges: classroom management and discipline, unmotivated students, underinvolved or adversarial parents, and tough working conditions. I hope this book helps you find solutions that work for you and the students in your school.

2

Classroom Management and Discipline

What Are the Challenges?

Most adults do not ever get a chance to experience the feeling of facing a group of 25 to 30 or more students who have *taken over*. They will never know the helplessness, powerlessness, and devastation of having to witness children bully their peers and even their teachers. Some people may have seen a version of classroom disorder on TV or in movies, but only some teachers and students have felt the chaos that prevails in many classrooms across our country.

The majority of 21st-century students have little respect for the kind of authority that was respected in times past, but, in most cases, teachers can handle these students without too much trouble. Classroom management and discipline may present a significant challenge, however, in schools where children come from poverty or dysfunctional families or communities. Too often, the troubled lives of these children interfere with their ability to function in the classroom and in society. They may bring their problems from home or neighborhood into the school.

One way to think about this kind of student misbehavior is to believe that certain children or young people have been damaged, perhaps by their families, their schools, their communities, and even by their country. These students have not thrived or matured as they should have because their environment has not met their needs. Most of the students who disrupt and destroy a learning environment exhibit these four deficiencies:

- ◆ Lack of respect for self, peers, and authority
- ◆ Lack of self-control and impulse control
- ◆ Inability to deal effectively with frustration or anger
- ◆ Lack of empathy

Some of these students have not progressed at a normal rate emotionally or ethically and their deficiencies can result in the following examples of disruptive behavior:

- ◆ Use of profanity and other disrespectful verbal responses to peers and teacher
- ◆ Arguing and bickering with students and teachers
- ◆ Blurting out or calling out inappropriately as a disruption of instruction
- ◆ Getting out of seat (or falling out of desk) to disrupt other students
- ◆ Not keeping hands and feet to self (i.e., tripping other students, horseplay)
- ◆ Fighting (physical and verbal)
- ◆ Chronic talking
- ◆ Gratuitous noisemaking (drumming on desk, whistling, fake sneezing or coughing)
- ◆ Destroying property (vandalism)
- ◆ Cheating on tests
- ◆ Passing notes, writing on desks, and other off task writing
- ◆ Racing and chasing in the building

I am sure many teachers could add to this list; however, these behaviors seem representative of the most common ones that erode learning environments, ruining learning opportunities for students and driving teachers from the classroom.

Another challenge for teachers concerning discipline makes this issue even more difficult. That challenge is *which discipline theory and practice to choose*. There is disagreement in what researchers and practitioners believe works best, and sometimes teachers are not sure what or who to believe. But first a word about the over-arching concept of classroom management.

Classroom Management

According to Robert Marzano (2003), classroom management can be divided into four subareas: "(1) establishing and enforcing rules and procedures, (2) carrying out disciplinary actions. (3) maintaining effective teacher and student relationships, and (4) maintaining an appropriate mental set for management" (pp. 88–89). These ideas are related to our discussion of discipline; therefore, I am using them to organize a presentation of research findings and resources that may be helpful to you as you deal with the discipline challenge. You may find that these ideas validate what you are already doing, or they may challenge you to evaluate your teaching style and practices. What follows are summaries of various findings and solutions. The headings are keyed to Marzano's subarea numbers:

Maintaining Effective Teacher and Student Relationships—Solutions

♦ Best classroom management is a combination of moderate dominance and moderate cooperation. In other words, teachers should not be too controlling or too permissive (Wubbels & Levy, 1993).

♦ One strategy does not fit all students; therefore, teachers should develop several helping skills to use with various students for various situations (Brophy, 1992).

♦ What follows are resources that suggest teachers use various strategies to deal with discipline issues:

"You Can Handle Them All" is a list of 116 behaviors; for example, the agitator, the complainer, and the class clown; with step-by-step strategies to deal with each of them. The source is Parents*Count,* online at http://parentscount.disciplinehelp.com/.

Discipline in the Secondary Classroom: A Problem-by-Problem Survival Guide by Randall S. Sprick (1985), offers a menu of problems with specific solutions.

Allen Mendler's *What Do I Do When…?* (1992) explains case studies showing how specific problems were solved with various strategies.

Here's How to Reach Me (2001), by Judith Pauley, Dianne Bradley, and Joseph Pauley, is a guide book with suggestions for dealing with the management of specific student types; for example the authors present ideas about how to deal with "Rosie Reactor (the Feeler)," "Will Workaholic (the Thinker)," "Paul Persister (the Believer)," "Doris Dreamer (the Imaginer)," and others.

Maintaining an Appropriate Mental Set for Management—Solutions

♦ The term "withitness" was coined by Jacob Kounin (1983), who discovered that teachers who constantly monitor behavior in the classroom and address it effectively prevent the escalation of misbehavior. Those teachers who seem to have eyes in the backs of their heads were most effective teachers (Brophy, 1996).

♦ Emotional objectivity (i.e., not taking students' behavior personally and reacting emotionally to it) allows teachers to better address students' misbehavior in a matter-of-fact manner. This does not mean that teachers should be aloof or unconcerned about misbehavior, it does mean, however, that an emotional reaction will decrease the teacher's ability to effectively deal with a problem, and it will interfere with the development of a positive relationship with students (Connolly, Dowd, Andrea, Nelson, & Tobias, 1998; Soar & Soar, 1979).

◆ To help you stay emotionally objective, you may need to remind yourself that most often students are not misbehaving as a personal response to you (Dreikurs, 1968). You can also learn from clinical psychologists, particularly Albert Ellis (1975), who conceptualized a psychotherapy technique called Rational Emotive Therapy. Ellis states that is not a behavior or action that causes us to have an emotion, it is what we believe about the behavior or action that causes the emotion. For instance, if we believe that students are misbehaving to make us miserable, we may become extremely angry or agitated. However, if we believe they are misbehaving for some reason other than to make us personally miserable, we may be able to change ("reframe") our beliefs about the behavior, and thus change our emotional response to that behavior. Also, if we believe a student is misbehaving because he has had no training or ability to act otherwise, we may see that we need to be understanding and instructive rather than punitive. This of course is easier said than done for people who have trouble controlling their emotions. Many people who have trouble controlling their emotions believe things *ought, must, or should* be a certain way, and if those things are not as they believe they ought, must or should be, then they are entitled to be upset. If you are having trouble in this area, you might want to work with someone who can help you get control of your emotions for your own sake and for the sake of your students.

Determining and Enforcing Rules and Procedures—Solutions

Most teachers develop a style of teaching that works best for them. Within that style, they should set forth clear expectations and procedures. Unclear rules and procedures can make teaching a challenge. Even small things like poor procedures for collecting students' work or for letting students leave the room to use the restroom, can disrupt the harmonious flow of the classroom. What follows is a discussion of classroom management styles that influence the development of rules and procedures, and suggestions for rules and procedures to help you deal with the challenge of classroom management.

Classroom Management Styles That Influence the Development of Rules and Procedures

This idea comes from the Center for Adolescent Studies associated with the University of Indiana. They have categorized teachers as having one of four classroom management styles as follows: authoritarian, authoritative, laissez-faire, and indifferent. The concepts—authoritarian, permissive, and authoritative—were first proposed as discipline styles by Baumrind (1978) and later as parenting styles by Baumrind (1991).

The following management inventory is adapted from one that was published in *Teacher Talk* in 1996 and is posted on the Internet by the Center for Adolescent Studies at www.indiana.edu/~cafs/tt/v1i2/what.html. You may choose to take this quick inventory to determine your basic classroom management style.

What Is Your Classroom Management Profile?
- ♦ Read each statement carefully.
- ♦ Write your response from the following scale:
  - 1 = Strongly disagree
  - 2 = Disagree
  - 3 = Neutral
  - 4 = Agree
  - 5 = Strongly Agree
- ♦ Respond to each statement based upon either actual or imagined classroom experience.
- ♦ Then, use the scoring instructions that follow the statements.
  1. If a student is disruptive during class, I assign him/her to detention, without further discussion.
  2. I don't want to impose any rules on my students.
  3. The classroom must be quiet in order for students to learn.
  4. I am concerned about both what my students learn and how they learn.
  5. If a student turns in a late homework assignment, it is not my problem.

---

6. I don't want to reprimand a student because it might hurt his/her feelings.

7. Class preparation isn't worth the effort.

8. I always try to explain the reasons behind my rules and decisions.

9. I will not accept excuses from a student who is tardy.

10. The emotional well-being of my students is more important than classroom control.

11. My students understand that they can interrupt my lecture if they have a relevant question.

12. If a student requests a hall pass, I always honor the request.

◆ To score your quiz, add your responses to statements in the following categories:

Statements 1, 3, and 9 refer to authoritarian style

Statements 4, 8, and 11 refer to authoritative style

Statements 6, 10, and 12 refer to laissez-faire style

Statements 2, 5, and 7 refer to indifferent style

◆ Your score could range from 3 to 15. The highest score indicates a strong preference for that style.

Descriptors for each style:

Authoritarian Teachers: Authoritarian teachers have firm control over the classroom. They may assign seats, have desks in rows, and may rarely allow students to leave the classroom. They require strict obedience to the rules and allow no disruption of teacher presentation. These teachers' rooms are quiet; however, students have few opportunities to learn from each other or practice communication skills. In the extreme, these teachers believe that students need only listen to their lecture to learn; therefore, they rarely plan activities like field trips and group work that distract students from the goals they have determined. These teachers give little indication that they care about their students.

Authoritative Teachers: Authoritative teachers place limits and controls on students, but also, at the same time, encourage their independence. They explain the reasons behind the rules, consider the circumstances for each discipline issue, and when addressing disruptive behavior, offer a polite but firm response. The environment in these classrooms allows students to practice communication skills. Authoritative teachers have a warm and caring attitude toward students, who they encourage to become self-reliant and socially competent. They act as a coach or guide in the learning process.

> *Laissez-faire Teachers:* Laissez-faire teachers put very few demands on their students. They allow students to disrupt teacher presentations and their discipline procedures are often inconsistent. These teachers want students to like them and they care more about the emotional well-being of students than the academic instruction. These teachers' style does not promote students' social competence and self-control. In the extreme, these teachers are overindulgent and permissive.
>
> *Indifferent Teachers:* Indifferent teachers put very little time into preparing for class. They often use the same lessons year after year. Very little learning occurs in theseteachers' classrooms because they do not control the class and do not provide opportunities for students to develop and practice skills. These teachers' classes are often a waste of time for students. These teachers are uninterested in the students and never plan activities such as field trips or special projects.

Suggestions for Rules and Procedures

One of the best sources of classroom procedural strategies is from Harry Wong's book, *The First Days of School* (1991). His book is a great tool for beginning teachers—and for veteran teachers if their procedural strategies are not working well. Wong offers ideas about how to handle literally everything a teacher needs to handle for the first days of school. Most importantly, he makes it clear that teachers can finish the day feeling rested and happy rather than worn-out and defeated. His strategies work! "Top 10 Management Procedures" contains my top 10 procedural suggestions (from Wong and others) that aid in classroom management.

Top 10 Management Procedures

Descriptor
Suggestion: Model and practice
Always model and practice everything you want students to do before you count on it working. This is especially helpful for "hands on" learners.
Suggestion: Have a "get quiet" signal
My favorite is this: I raise my hand, and then students raise their hands as we all get quiet. The purpose of students' raising their hands is that it is easier to spread the signal because a student may see another student's hand, but not the teacher's. Other methods include clapping and getting a clapping back response, cutting the lights, and ringing a bell or sounding a buzzer. You could rotate signals or choose different signals for different occasions.
Suggestion: Passing class work papers to the teacher
Pass from wall to wall rather than from back to front, as follows: Tell students that time is up, and they must turn in their work. Next, tell them to pass their papers from the left wall (show left with your hands) to the right wall (show with your hands). Tell them that on the count of three, they should pass their papers without talking or making any noise. Tell them that you will count to 10 as they pass, and then collect all the papers that made it to the end of the row. Papers that did not make it in time to the end of the row will not be graded. (Unless there are extenuating circumstances—for instance, I have had students maliciously hold other students' papers so that they would receive a zero.) Other options: Have OUT boxes and IN boxes—Ask students to place work in boxes as they come into the room. This idea is great for homework.
Suggestion: Time limits
Make sure students have time limits for class work or they will take as long as you give them to do the work. Do not worry if some students do not finish at first. They will learn that they may not get off task or waste time.
Suggestion: Supplies
If you teach underprivileged students, you need to be prepared to provide supplies for them that simply will not be provided on a regular basis from the home. Pencils—Ask students to trade you a shoe or something they will not forget to get back so that you may get your pencil back. Many teachers have a box or can of pencils from which students may borrow, but often the supply gets totally depleted. Another suggestion is to buy a box of golf

pencils. Paper—Provide unlined paper. Students prefer lined paper and will try harder to remember to keep a supply. Tissues—Do not count on students to bring tissues from home even if they know they will need them at school because they have a cold. They will not remember to get toilet paper from the bathroom either. You may have to think of your classroom as a home in which you need to supply your visitors with certain essentials, like tissue, or you will spend too much energy fighting that battle. Ask volunteers to bring in tissue or buy it yourself; however, do not give grades or points to students for bringing it. This is unfair and unethical because students should not be allowed to buy grades.

Suggestion: Restroom breaks

Unless a student has a disorder, most children and young people have very efficient bladders. They need to plan to use the restroom at times other than the middle of class. If they have to use the restroom in the middle of the class, it should be allowed only as an emergency. If a child has more than one emergency per quarter, he is possibly just trying to get out of class. Allow only one emergency bathroom pass per quarter. Keep track of this in your grade book or your policy is a sham. Always allow students with special situations to use the restroom as needed.

Suggestion: Rules and expectations

Make just a few classroom rules such as be respectful in all you say and do, raise your hand to talk or to get out of your seat, keep your hands and feet to yourself, stay on task and do all of your work. Clearly articulate that your expectations are high and never belie those words. Be consistent!

Suggestion: Sponge activities

Have a repertoire of sponge activities that absorb time so that students are always in engaged. My favorites for those who finish before the time limit: (1) take out a book and read silently, (2) help me give out materials, (3) work on an ongoing project. If the entire class finishes before the bell, I usually play a game related to a review of what we have been studying. I like a version of Around the World (students challenge each other to answer questions to see who can stay standing until the bell rings). There are excellent websites for sponge activities. My favorite is online at tepserver.ucsd.edu/courses/tep129/Educational Sponges.pdf.

Suggestion: Focusing

Always have an interesting way to focus students' attention at the beginning of class. Best focus activities relate in some way to the previous day's work or to an objective on which you will be working during the class. Favorite focusing activities: (1) Five-question quiz—as review or to preassess level of knowledge. (To grade the quiz give an A+ for all right answers, a B+ for 1 wrong, a C for 2 wrong, a C– for 3 wrong, a D for 4 wrong and an F for all wrong. Do not grade the quiz if it is a preassessment of knowledge of a topic before it is introduced.) (2) An interesting writing prompt for a journal. (3) A picture that inspires a writing prompt. Rule: Always make sure you have students' attention before you begin instruction.

Suggestion: Helpers

Let children and young people have as much responsibility as possible as helpers in the classroom. Give everyone a chance to be a helper.

Classroom management solutions can be easy to implement and can help you avoid getting into power struggles or other conflicts with students that might escalate into discipline issues. What follows is a discussion of discipline issues and how our culture is divided about how to deal with them.

Carrying out Disciplinary Actions

As you read about suggestions for ways to carry out disciplinary actions, keep in mind your own values and what would best fit your situation. I discuss discipline issues in the following sequence: (1) overview of opposing ideas, (2) chart that shows on which side of the debate specific discipline programs fit, (3) evaluation of opposing views using the BESST Criterion, (4) example of using the Five Pause Points to solve a discipline challenge, (5) suggestions for dealing with your own school system, and (6) special disciplinary actions for children of poverty.

Overview of the Opposing Ideas

Disciplinary action is one of the more complicated aspects of classroom management, and, unfortunately for teachers, theorists and practitioners are in conflict about what works best. Some theorists believe the teacher (or other authorities, such as administrators) should be in charge. Other theorists believe in a form of collaborative classroom control. A smoothly running classroom requires cooperation among teachers, administrators, students, and parents. The teacher functions as a facilitator or coach who inspires students by aligning teaching closely with students' goals and needs.

Where Specific Discipline Programs Fit—Solutions

The "Discipline Chart" shows on which side of the issue specific discipline programs fit in terms of control. Programs on the left reflect the idea that students can be trusted to behave with looser teacher controls; the programs on the right reflect the idea that the teacher must be in firm control of the class if students are to behave appropriately. Although there are many other programs that help teachers and administrators devise discipline procedures, those listed here seem to be the most useful and popular. The "Discipline Chart" contains the briefest of information about the opposing views. See the Discipline Chart Overviews on the following pages for overviews that give you a sense of what each program might offer you in the way of solutions to your discipline problems. The challenge for you is to decide which of these programs, if any, you might want to learn to use.

Discipline Chart

Teacher Trusts Students to Share Control of the Class	Teacher is in Firm Control of the Class
1. Jane Nelson Positive Discipline	2. Lee and Marlene Canter Assertive Discipline
3. Allen Mendler Discipline with Dignity	4. Connolly, Dowd, Andrea, Nelson, and Tobias The Boys Town Model
5. Marvin Marshall Discipline without Stress, Punishment, or Rewards	6. The Honor System

See the "Discipline Chart Overviews" on the following pages for overviews that give you a sense of what each program might offer you in the way of solutions to your discipline problems. The challenge for you is to decide which of these programs, if any, you might want to learn to use.

Discipline Chart Overivews

Teacher Trusts Students to Share Control of Class
1. *Jane Nelson (Positive Discipline)*[1] Based on the work of Alfred Adler (1870–1937) and Rudolf Dreikurs (1897–1972), Positive Discipline was conceptualized by Jane Nelson and others in the 1980s. The underlying belief within this method is that children who feel valued as members of their community will be less likely to misbehave. This discipline method trains teachers to help students learn important social and life skills in an atmosphere of respectfulness and collaboration. One of the key elements of this program is "the classroom meeting" during which students discuss and make decisions about important classroom issues. The "Four Criteria for Effective Discipline" according to this model are as follows: 1. Helps children feel a sense of connection. (Belonging and significance) 2. Is mutually respectful and encouraging. (Kind and firm at the same time) 3. Is effective long-term. (Considers what the child is thinking, feeling, learning, and deciding about himself and his world—and what to do in the future to survive and thrive.) 4. Teaches important life skills. (Respect, concern for others, problem solving, and cooperation as well as the skills to contribute to the home, school or larger community.) Training for this includes teachers, parents and students learning the following tools and concepts: ◆ Mutual respectfulness ◆ Understanding the belief behind the behavior ◆ Encouragement rather than praise ◆ Solutions rather than punishment ◆ Problem solving techniques Instructional discipline that is neither permissive nor punitive ◆ Learning experientially ◆ Parent education programs ◆ Inexpensive training that is expanding through networking

Teacher Is In Firm Control of the Class

2. *Lee and Marlene Canter (Assertive Discipline)*[2]

Assertive discipline is a common-sense model of discipline based on the research and practice associated with assertiveness training and applied behavior analysis. Lee and Marlene Canter developed the model when they were invited to help a school system get control over their students. They developed a "teacher-in-charge" management system that is possibly the most widely used behavior management program to date. Assertive discipline promotes the following concepts: Teachers should have a few clearly stated rules that are reinforced by rewarding those who comply and by giving negative consequences to those who do not. Teachers should work confidently and quickly to resolve/address issues created by students who disobey the rules. Teachers should give firm, clear, and concise messages to all students. Teachers should not develop adversarial relationships with students nor should they react in a hostile or aggressive manner towards students. It is in students' best interest that the teacher is firmly in control of the class. Allowing students to misbehave is not in their best interest nor is it supportive of society's expectations. Teachers have a right to expect support from parents and administrators. Assertive teachers are demanding yet warm, supportive, and respectful of all students. This technique should be implemented by taking the following steps:

1. Believe that there is no *acceptable* reason for misbehavior.

2. Decide what rules you need to implement.

3. Plan negative consequences for noncompliance with your rules. You must be consistent in using these consequences.

4. Determine a discipline hierarchy in which consequences get increasingly punitive and/or restrictive.

5. Plan positive consequences for acceptable behavior. Use verbal praise as well as prizes and written praise.

6. Explain the rules to students in a meeting.

7. Instruct students to write the rules and ask them to get their parents to sign them.

8. Start the program as soon as you can.

9. Learn communication skills that will help you speak to students assertively about their behavior.

Teacher Trusts Students to Share Control of Class

3. *Allen Mendler and Richard Curwin (Discipline with Dignity)*[3]
Allen Mendler proposes that children in our current society are quite different from those in the past; most of them no longer respect or fear authority. Therefore, the "obedience model" of discipline no longer works with them. He and his colleague Richard Curwin, with whom he devceloped this philosophy, believe that most teachers, many of whom grew up under an obedience model, still rely on that model for discipline strategies, and they have few or *no* alternative strategies to maintain order in the classroom. Mendler and Curwin adamantly defend the right of each child to be treated with dignity no matter what their response to authority. Mendler believes there is a significant difference between consequences and punishments, and believes that natural consequences are far superior to punishment, which can often be disrespectful of the child who is being punished. He shows a clear relationship among stress, motivation, teaching practices, and discipline issues, and offers countless strategies that help teachers solve specific and generic classroom management/discipline issues. These authors believe that all children need the following:

- To feel and believe they are capable and successful
- To know others care about them.
- To realize that they are able to influence people and events.
- To remember and practice helping others through their own generosity.
- To have fun and stimulation.

Mendler believes that the behavior modification techniques used in many schools make students dependent on the person who is "shaping" their behavior. He believes that teachers who insist on making their students "Do it my way or else!" embarrass and humiliate students and make some students hate school and learning. They believe that teachers who control students' behavior through rewards and punishments make their students dependent on authority figures to tell them how to behave. And unfortunately it seems that these children do not internalize the value of responsible behavior. In other words, they only behave when they are manipulated by an authority figure. One of the major issues this author addresses is helping students understand that they have an "internal locus of control" and that they do not have to feel they are victims of others' actions or words. In addition, this author has a list of "7 Principles of Effective Discipline" as follows:

1. Use long-term behavior changes vs. short term quick fixes. People take time!
2. Stop doing ineffective things. Some discipline issues defy common sense.

3. I will be fair, and I won't always treat everyone the same. Tailor the consequence to the child.

4. Rules must make sense.

5. Model what you expect.

6. Responsibility is more important than obedience.

7. Always treat students with dignity.

Finally, he has a criteria for using any discipline method as follows:

- It must work to stop disruptive behavior and/or build constructive, prosocial behavior.
- You (the teacher) would find the method acceptable if you were on the receiving end. Use yourself and your feelings as a guide to the relative emotional benefits or liabilities of any and all methods.
- The method(s) are geared toward teaching responsibility (better decision making) even when obedience is necessary (i.e., safety).
- You are willing to model the method, not merely preach it.
- You can identify and explain how following a rule or procedure can provide both immediate and long-term benefits.
- The method is compatible with the seven principles of Effective Discipline.

Teacher Is In Firm Control of the Class

4. The Boys Town Model (*Social Learning Theory*) (Connolly, Dowd, Andreas, Nelson, & Tobias)

The Boys Town Model is based on applied behavior analysis and social learning theory, which states that behavior is learned through feedback and environmental consequences. The proponents of this model believe that behavior occurs as part of a contingency. They describe a contingency as having these three parts:

- Antecedents: aspects of the environment that occur before a behavior
- Behaviors: what a person says or does in relationship to the antecedent.
- Consequences: what happens as the result of a behavior

This model states that teachers can help students change their behaviors by manipulating antecedents, consequences, or both. Similar to the behaviorists, they believe educators can shape the behavior of their students. In terms of punishment and praise this model offers the following rationales:

- Suppressing behavior through coercion has only a temporary effect.
- *Assertive discipline methods result in counter-aggression from students.
- Acknowledging appropriate behavior through effective praise encourages appropriate behavior.

There are four steps to appropriate praise as follows:
1. Describe the appropriate behavior.
2. Explain your rationale for praising the behavior.
3. Request that the student acknowledge your praise.
4. Provide a positive consequence (e.g., 10 extra minutes of free time).
The Boys Town Social Skills Curriculum includes the following:
1. Following instructions
2. Accepting criticism or a consequence
3. Accepting "No" for an answer
4. Greeting others
5. Getting the teacher's attention
6. Making a request
7. Disagreeing appropriately
8. Giving criticism
9. Resisting peer pressure
10. Making an apology
11. Engaging in conversation
12. Giving compliments
13. Accepting compliments
14. Volunteering
15. Reporting other youth's behavior
16. Introducing yourself
Besides the Social Skills Curriculum, the Boys Town model also includes training in the following areas: teacher interactions, a motivation system, and administrative intervention.

Teacher Trusts Students to Share Control of Class

5. Marvin Marshall (*Discipline Without Stress, Punishment, or Rewards*)[5]
Marvin Marshall bases his strategies significantly on the work of William Glasser (1986, 1990). He, like Glasser, believes that behavior is a choice and that students must be coached to make choices that improve the classroom, the home, and the community. He believes that teachers can feel less stress as they are teaching if they begin to see that they cannot *make* a student behave; they can only facilitate growth toward self-control and responsibility.
Marshall offers clear rationales for why punishments and rewards go against best discipline practices. He provides step-by-step guides for shifting responsibility from the teacher or authority to students. He clearly details how to teach students *The Raise Responsibility System* in which students learn the *ABCD's of the Levels of Development*.

He suggests teachers use a method that involves students defining and drawing pictures of the following concepts:

A = Anarchy, the absence of rules and authority

B = Bullying or bossing, which he expands to include students' disruptive behavior (such as calling out answers or disturbing others) as bullying behavior (i.e., bullying the teacher and bullying those students who are trying to learn from that teacher)

These two letters are levels of behavior "below the line." They are unacceptable and require the teacher to go to the B level also in order to become a "boss" for the student who is not conforming to the expectations set up in the class.

C = Conformity and cooperation, which is complying with teachers requests to do the right thing

D = Democracy, which is expanded to include behaving appropriately because it is the right thing to do

These two letters are above the line and acceptable.

Marshall's consequences for students who choose behavior below the line is that that they should be required to write a reflective essay for the first offence. The first offence is a warning and parents are not contacted. However, for second, third, and even fourth offences, students are required to fill out a self-diagnostic referral form and their parents are contacted. After the third self-diagnostic referral, Marshall suggests a disciplinary referral and parent conference. For students whose misbehavior is chronic, Marshall suggests that a teacher may want to write an office referral in which the student's name and infraction is filled out but not dated. The child learns that if he chooses to behave, he will avoid that referral.

Dr. Marshall also promotes the classroom meeting. He outlines the procedures of a typical classroom meeting as follows:

(1) defining the topic,

(2) personalizing the topic, and

(3) challenging the students to solve the problem presented.

He suggests that meetings should be held weekly and last about 10 minutes for younger students and 20 minutes for older students. Marshall also offers suggestions to help parents with their relationships with their children.

Teacher Is In Firm Control of the Class

6. *The Honor Level System*[6]

Based on the moral development theory of Lawrence Kohlberg (1981), this system combines assertive discipline with empathy and understanding of where students are in their ethical development. The authors of this idea believe that just as students perform at different levels in content areas, they also perform at different levels when it comes to discipline. The program acknowledges that many students have not reached the level of ethical maturity that would allow them to make mature choices. They categorize students into four stages as follows:

Stage 1: This is the Power Stage where might makes right. If children do not grow out of this stage in early childhood, they become very difficult older students. They are often aggressive and oppositional. They have few rules of their own, but may obey others' rules out of fear of punishment.

Stage 2: This is the Rewards and Punishment Stage where students are looking for "what's in it for me?" Students should grow out of this stage by age eight or nine; however, if they do not outgrow this stage, they respond best to assertive teachers who provide constant supervision. Without supervision (e.g., in the halls) or with less assertive teachers, these students can be difficult to control.

Stage 3: In this stage, which is typically a middle-school or junior-high stage, students want to do what is right to please the teacher or other authority figure. These students are beginning to trust others and to build relationships and they need gentle reminders to keep them in line. An overly assertive teacher can make students in this stage flip back to Stage 2.

Stage 4: This is the stage of self-discipline. Students behave because it is the right thing to do to promote social order. These students rarely get into trouble and they can be excellent role models for others. The Disciplinary Levels (which are assessed every 14 days) are as follows:

Honor Level One: Students rarely get into trouble. To stay at this level, students must have no incidents of detention or time out within the 14-day period. They are rewarded through events planned by the school, such as extended breaks and recreational activities. They also receive impromptu rewards, such as free ice cream or surprise activities. In many schools about 70% to 80% of students are at this level.

Honor Level Two: These students may have had only one or two problems within the 14-day period. They receive privileges and rewards similar to Honor Level One students. About 20% to 30% of students are on this level.

Honor Level Three: These students get into trouble more often. They may have three or more consequences for misbehaving within the 14-day period. These students do not receive the privileges and rewards received by Honor Levels One and Two. They might negotiate to be involved in some activities. These students account for about 5% of the student body.

Honor Level Four: These are the students who are always in trouble. They never have special privileges and may not negotiate to become involved, as do the Level Threes.

This system uses the following consequences:

Infraction	Consequence	Infraction	Consequence
1st	15-minute noon detention	4th	In-school suspension
2nd	30-minute noon detention	5th	Saturday school
3rd	After-school detention	6th	Suspension from school

1. From "What is Positive Discipline," www.positivediscipline.com/What_is_Positive_Discipline.html.
2. From "Assertive Discipline," http://maxweber.hunter.cuny.edu/pub/eres/EDSPC715_MCINTYRE/AssertiveDiscipline.html.
3. From Allen N. Mendler (1992), *What Do I Do When...?*
4. From Connolly, Dowd, Andreas, Nelson, & Tobias (1995) *The Well Managed Classroom: Promoting Student Success Through Social Skills Instruction.*
5. From Marvin L. Marshall (2001), *Discipline Without Stress, Punishments, or Rewards.*
6. From "Overview [Discipline by Design]," http://honorlevel.com/x83.xml.

Evaluation of Opposing Views Using the BESST Criterion = Value Added

If you are trying to decide which classroom management or discipline concepts or perspectives are *right,* or which one or ones resonate with your worldview, you may want to consider all of the above ideas within the framework of the BESST Criterion = Value Added. I will model for you how I decided which side of the discipline debate was best for my situation. Here is a copy of "BESST Criterion = Value Added" and my analysis.

BESST Criterion = Value Added

Brain-Based	Ethical	Standards	Systems Theory
In an environment where students' goals are aligned with classroom experiences, the brain motivates itself to learn without being bribed by rewards or threatened by punishment.	All people (including children) are created equal with equal rights to freedom, happiness, and the Golden Rule.	Extensive skills and knowledge help teachers provide a positive learning environment.	Having an awareness of the interactions that make up an environment helps teachers respectfully and strategically plan their actions.

♦ *Brain-Based:* Bribery and punishment do not work according to brain-based research. Acknowledging or celebrating accomplishments and using fair consequences to address poor behavior *are* aligned with brain-based research. Any program that promotes a punitive, stressful environment is not good for students or teachers. Looking at the chart that outlines the six programs you will notice that the practices on the right involve some kind of reward and punishment routine that necessitates a *power-over* philosophy. The practices on the left rely on respect for authority by virtue of role as well as because the authority has earned respect.

♦ *Ethics:* All of the practices claim to be respectful; however, the practices on the right seem to be stuck at the "conventional level" of ethical development because they require an authority to assure the well-functioning of a class, school or district. These practices do not seem to trust that mutual respect can be achieved. They believe that for discipline to be maintained, the leader must be in control of the situation. The practices on the left support the idea that students can be trusted with sharing authority for discipline issues.

♦ *Standards:* It is clear from this challenge that knowledge and skill is critical if teachers want to have well-disciplined classrooms. The standards movement does not support disrespectful programs that might be insensitive to the needs of students. They insist that all programs maintain the dignity of students no matter what they have done.

♦ If a teacher wants to maintain a well-functioning classroom, he needs to master classroom management techniques that work for him. These techniques would include giving students choices within a framework of respectfulness and kindness, and addressing poor behavior with instructive consequences rather than revenge seeking punishments. The more a teacher knows about his students and the techniques that work with them, the smoother his classroom will run. The skills involved with maintaining a well-disciplined classroom take practice and support. It can take several years for a teacher to obtain the knowledge and skills necessary to facilitate a well-functioning classroom. In the meantime, administrators and peers should provide support, training, and ongoing coaching to assist novice teachers about classroom management and discipline. The biggest problem for some teachers is they do not fully learn what it takes to meet the standards because other teachers and administrators do not know how to help them. For this reason, many districts are developing coaching positions to help struggling teachers. These coaches, unlike administrators, do not evaluate teachers' work; therefore, teachers can more easily admit that they need help. Well-trained coaches and mentors can help struggling teachers grow into the profession.

♦ Systems Theory: The programs described in the chart leave out the importance of implementing that program within a school system. This disregard of the system may explain why some teachers and schools do not succeed in implementing a discipline program.

♦ = Added Value: Although some teachers may feel more comfortable with more control over students' behavior to keep their rooms "in order," this control does not add value to the students' learning to function as responsible citizens of our world. The discipline procedures that expect students to control themselves in the classroom, add value to their lives as citizens in the class and citizens of the future. This knowledge adds tremendous value to the lives of teachers who can relax and enjoy the marvelous world of a classroom that hums with harmony and glows with excitement that only learning can produce.

Based on the BESST Criterion and your own ideas, which theories and practices seem most useful to you? Here follows an example of how to use the Five Pause-Point Decision-Making System when dealing with a discipline issue.

Five Pause-Point Decision-Making System With a Discipline Issue

P1—Planning an Action: It was nearing the end of the year in a class I taught some time ago. I was concerned with the amount of disrespectful blurting (speaking out) behavior my students continued to exhibit. My plan was to prevail upon my students' sense of fairness and respectfulness and to ask them to determine consequences for blurting. When I planned to present this idea to my students, I thought about these questions:

1. Was my action in line with brain-based research? For instance did I need to use bribery or punishment and were my goals aligned with students' goals?

   Appealing to my students' sense of fairness helped me avoid bribery or punishment. As long as students had choices about addressing the behaviors, I was able to avoid attempting to control their behavior through reward of punishment. I could facilitate their designing an appropriate consequence.

2. Would I hurt anyone or help anyone if I asked the students to determine the consequences for blurting?

   These students were hurting me with their disrespect and being enabled to blurt was hurting them also, so that doing something to inspire them to take more ownership of this problem might actually help them. It was also bothering me to be in the role of constant "enforcer." I was disappointed that all my other strategies for ending the blurting had not been totally successful for everyone. (Interestingly one of the worst offenders did not blurt during this class, so I think my work with her may have had some success.)

3. Was this action in line with the standards? Did it show skill and knowledge and create a positive atmosphere for learning?

   Being able to facilitate the process of shared decision making demonstrates skill in creating a positive atmosphere for learning. It also demonstrates knowledge of human growth and development in that I understand how students need to take ownership of an issue in order to deal effectively with it.

4. Was my action sensitive to the system it affected?

This classroom system was a difficult one because all of the students were challenged learners. Many of them were extremely hyperactive and had difficulty focusing on tasks and maintaining reasonable self-control. In order to design an effective intervention with them, I needed to keep in mind their limitations and readiness to take more responsibility for behaving well.

5. What did I do?

I challenged the class to determine a consequence for blurting.

P2—Implementation/Observation: I implemented the plan of asking the class to determine the consequences for blurting. I observed their reactions and this is what happened: They came up with four ideas: If you blurt—(1) no computer, (2) no Internet access, (3) write an essay about blurting, or (4) write 1,000 times "I will not blurt in class." No Computer won and four students promptly tested the consequences. I did not let them use a computer, and I sent them to the library with an alternative assignment instead. I sent them to the library because I was concerned it they stayed in the room they would continue to blurt out.

P3—Reflection:

1. Did I need to use bribery or punishment?

   I did not need bribery or punishment because the consequences were predetermined and no one seemed to feel they were treated unfairly. No one was bribed because the class had determined the consequences.

2. Did I help anyone or hurt anyone?

   I wondered if I should have encouraged the class to determine an alternative to the no-computer rule because I still had to make the decision about what to do if a student could not use a computer. Sending students to the media center instead of staying in class might have been a faulty alternative to no-computer because some students might have considered it a treat to go to the media center; in other words, the consequence was better than behaving appropriately. I was concerned that the other students would notice that the consequence of no computer was not that bad because the offending students got to go to the library, but no one complained or said, "I'd rather go to the library too." I was not intending to be punitive; however, so the consequence of going to the media center seemed logical, though not perfect. It turned out that getting to stay in the class *was* a better alternative than going to the library. We had a very pleasant class for most of the period, and when the offenders returned, they saw that we were playing a rhyming game that was very popular. I may have helped the whole class take ownership of the blurting problem, but I would not find more information until I continued the policy in future classes.

3. Did I demonstrate knowledge and skill?

I demonstrated knowledge that giving students choices and having them take ownership for problems is better than dictating rules. I used my knowledge of teaching strategies when I used the activity (the game) students enjoy. I used skill in implementing the class consequences for dealing with blurting behavior.

4. Did I consider the system I was affecting?

By showing the offenders that they missed a good time, I was letting the system have an impact on the offenders rather than doing anything specific myself. When the offenders noticed it might be more beneficial to stay in the room, they may have seen a reason to control their blurting behavior. That memory may help them in the future when they are making a decision about blurting, if their hyperactivity allows them a chance to think before they act.

5. What did I do?

I decided to try the no-computer consequence for next class to notice if fewer students would test it.

P4—Revision: I decided to see what happened rather than revising my plans at this point.

P5—Acting With More Knowledge—Value Added: As students entered the room, I reminded them that the class had voted on a no-computer consequence for blurting. I admonished them all to be careful. This is what I observed: Only three students blurted this time, and none of them were offenders from last class period. I sent these students to the media center, but this time I had a problem. These three offenders caused problems in the media center; therefore, I had a pleasant conversation with the media specialist, and we decided to bring an alternative (to the computers) to my classroom, so that she would not be stuck with the offenders, and I could monitor their work. Even though the number of blurting offenders decreased by only one, I continued to enforce the no-computer rule made by the class. I think I got the students' attention. For instance, one student corrected his classmate for blurting during our class. Based on my decision to implement this plan of action, I have added value to my abilities to use shared decision making in the classroom and have added value to my students' lives because I facilitated their taking responsibility for behaving appropriately.

Suggestions for Dealing With Your Own School System—Solutions

If your classroom discipline system is not working for the reasons stated in the previous section or if you have other reasons, think about the problem from the following perspectives.

- ♦ Yourself

  - Think of yourself as a leader in the systems in which you work.

  - Choose the classroom management strategy or strategies you think will work for you. Learn more about how to use that strategy or those strategies.

  - Get help to practice the strategy or strategies. Remember, just understanding a strategy and believing it is a good idea will not make it work. Implementing many of these ideas takes practice and may require help from a supportive and skilled colleague or mentor.

- ♦ Students

  - Find out students' reasons for misbehaving and work strategically to find the right strategy to promote change. As stated at the beginning of the chapter, some students from dysfunctional systems have the following core issues: disrespect of self and others, little or no self-control, no empathy, and anger issues.

  - If your students or the system in which you work is dependent on reward and punishment to control behavior, meet students and the system where it is. Rather than bribing them to behave, you may be able to model for students the concepts of celebrating successes and encouraging good behavior. Rather than punishing them for their mistakes, you may also choose to rely on natural consequences and strategies to raise students into higher levels of responsibility. However, if your system is not at this level, you should be respectful of where your administrators and fellow teachers are functioning. You might show them how your ideas work, but you should avoid criticizing them for their belief and behaviors.

  - You may also need to understand as much as possible about the family systems students bring to school each day.

- Do what you can to help students deal with their family system by teaching them coping skills that might help them out of a bad situation.
- Instill in them the belief that education is the way out of a dysfunctional system.

◆ Parents

- Provide regular and frequent two-way communication with students' parents about good and bad behavior.
- Welcome parents into your school and classroom. Ask them to help you with some aspect of your curriculum. Engage them in your classroom procedures as much as possible.
- Ask parents for feedback about your classroom management and discipline plans.

◆ Administration

- Encourage administrators to involve teachers in decisions about school rules and procedures.
- Volunteer to help determine rules and procedures.
- Communicate regularly and often with administrators about classroom management issues. Tell them about your successes as well as your concerns.
- Offer to provide support and mentoring to teachers who are struggling with classroom management.
- If your administrative team has not heard of an interesting classroom management strategy, give them an executive summary of the information or copy an article for them. If you can get their time, talk to them about why you like the concept and how your school might implement it.

◆ Community

- Learn who or what organizations make important decisions about school funding, policies, and procedures.
- Join with other advocacy groups or work on your own to inform those decision makers about how their funding, policies, and procedures translate into challenges in your classroom and/or school.
- Invite policy makers into your school to see for themselves.

If you are attempting to change a system, you must remember to approach that system respectfully in order to develop a common ground from which to leverage change. Also, make sure you remember that if *you* change, the system will change, but you may not be prepared for what happens in response to your change.

Finally, some members of the system may reject or resist your leadership, but don't give up if you believe you are right, just try another route. You never know what will make an idea take off or *tip*. The idea of the *tipping point* is that sometimes what we think will move an idea or solve a problem has no effect, but the *right* thing said to the *right* person or persons at the *right* time, may totally reverse a problem or promote an idea.

Special Disciplinary Actions for Children of Poverty— Challenges and Solutions

Poverty has its own set of circumstances that are not widely understood by teachers who have come from middle class backgrounds. We cannot forget about issues of poverty when we address classroom management and discipline. Ruby Payne in her book, *A Framework for Understanding Poverty* (1998), has contributed greatly to our understanding of how poverty can affect the way some children deal with their teachers and fellow students. "Payne Strategies" is a summary of some of her strategies.

Payne Strategies

Behavior Related to Poverty	Causes	Intervention
Laugh when disciplined	A way to save face in matriarchal poverty	Understand the reason for the behavior. Tell students three or four other behaviors that would be more appropriate.
Argue loudly with the teacher	Poverty is participatory, and the culture has a distrust of authority. See the system as inherently dishonest and unfair.	Don't argue with the students. Have students write the answers to questions, such as "What did you do?" "When you did that, what did you want?" "List four other things you could have done." What will you do next time?"

Angry response	Anger is based on fear. Question what the fear is: loss of face?	Respond in the adult voice (as opposed to child or parent voice). When students cool down, discuss other responses they could have used.
Cannot follow directions	Little procedural memory used in poverty. Sequence not used or valued.	Write steps on the board. Have them write at the top of the paper the steps needed to finish the task. Have them practice procedural self-talk.
Extremely disorganized	Lack of planning, scheduling, or prioritizing skills. Not taught in poverty. Also probably don't have a place at home to put things so that they can be found.	Teach a simple, color-coded method of organization in the classroom. Use the five-finger method for memory at the end of the day. Have each student give a plan for organization.
Complete only part of a task	No procedural self-talk. Do not "see" the whole task.	Write on the board all the parts of the task. Require each student to check off each part when finished.
Disrespectful to teacher	Have a lack of respect for authority and the system. May not know any adults worthy of respect.	Tell students that disrespect is not a choice. Identify for students the correct voice tone and word choice that are acceptable. This allows students to practice.
Harm other students verbally or physically	This may be a way of life. Probably a way to buy space or distance. May have become a habitual response. Poverty tends to address issues in the negative.	Tell students that aggression is not a choice. Have students generate other options that are appropriate at school. Give students phrases that can be used instead of the one(s) used.

Cheat or steal	Indicative of weak support system, weak role models/emotional resources. May indicate extreme financial need. May indicate little instruction/guidance during formative years.	Use a metaphor story to find the reason or need behind the cheating or stealing. Address the reason or need. Emphasize that the behavior is illegal and not an option at school
Talk incessantly	Poverty is very participatory.	Have students write all questions and responses on a note card two days a week. Tell students that each gets five comments a day. Build participatory activities into the lesson.
Inappropriate or vulgar comments	Reliance on casual register; may not know formal register.	Have students generate (or teach other students) phrases that could be used to say the same thing.
Physically fight	Necessary to survive in poverty. Only know the language of survival. Do not have language or belief system to use conflict resolution. See themselves as less than a man or woman if they do not fight.	Stress that fighting is unacceptable in school. Examine other options that students could live with at school other than fighting. One option is not to settle the business at school, for example.
Hands always on someone else	Poverty has a heavy reliance on nonverbal data and touch.	Allow them to draw or doodle. Have them hold their hands behind their back when in line or standing. Give them as much to do with their hands as possible in a constructive way.

Summary

Classroom management and discipline challenges can drive teachers from the classroom. Just deciding which theories and practices to choose can be a huge challenge, especially for novice teachers. It takes some teachers more time than others to understand how to master these challenges. Those who have mastered them should do everything they can to offer support and coaching to those who are struggling.

3

Unmotivated Students

What Are the Challenges?

One of the saddest challenges a teacher can face is the issue of unmotivated students. Some of these students have learned helplessness or have completely shut down all enthusiasm for learning. Some will work for teachers they like and do nothing for those they do not like. Lack of motivation accounts for poor achievement and can even lead students to drop out of school altogether. The unmotivated student is a sad problem, but one that might be remedied more easily than the other challenges. Unfortunately, traditional teaching practices often *create* the problem of unmotivated students. Teachers, rather than looking at their own ineffective practices, often blame the victims of those poor teaching practices, their students. As with our other topics, there is not always agreement about why students become unmotivated, nor is there agreement about what to do when students become unmotivated; therefore, it becomes challenging to determine which theories and practices to use to guide your solutions.

I discuss these challenges in this chapter, arranging the discussion as follows: (1) Edward Deci's self-system, which explains why we do what we do, (2) What do students say motivates them? (3) Teaching styles that create motivation issues, (4) Teaching practices that are best in terms of motivation, (5) Evaluating opposing views based on the BESST Criterion, (6) Using the five pause-points for decision making in a student motivation example, (7) Other issues that address the challenge of student motivation, and (8) Suggestions for dealing with your own school system.

(1) Edward Deci's Self-System— Why We Do What We Do

Edward Deci's book *Why We Do What We Do* (1995) provides one of the best discussions I found on the concept of motivation. Though his conclusions seem counterintuitive, his experiments (which have been proved by brain-based research) are irrefutable. Deci says that the traditional view, that people are motivated by rewards, praise, punishments, or competition, has not had the expected results. In a startling experiment, he shows that paying people to do something that they enjoy doing can interfere with or destroy the pleasure of doing it.

One of Deci's most useful discussions is about how control affects motivation. He says that it is the nature of most human beings to want to feel autonomous (governed by self); they do not want to be controlled by outside pressures or by other people. The issue of control becomes highly important in relationships where the ability to control is unequal. For instance, teacher-pupil relationships can be thought of as *one-up* (teacher) and *one-down* (student). In these relationships, if the person in the one-up position wants to have a positive impact on the person who is one-down, he or she must create the illusion that the one-down person has autonomy. In the state of nature, the child who is growing and developing must convert the external messages he gets from those in one-up positions into internal messages that form the self. The best way for the teacher to accomplish the goal of motivating growing children is to allow them to make their own choices within limits. If choices are limited, the motivating teacher can at least show she understands the child's perspective. For instance, if a teacher wants her students to participate in activities that are not typically enjoyable, she must show the students that she understands why they would not enjoy the activity. As long as teachers identify with students' perspectives, they can usually help them accept responsibility for choosing the right behaviors and internalizing them.

Deci states that there are only two types of responses to external control: compliance and defiance. Students can choose either behavior, but both are responses to external control. For students to internalize behaviors, the behaviors must either be *introjected* from an outside source or they may be *integrated* (or consumed) by the persons themselves. Integrated behaviors become part of the person's self and add to his/her sense of autonomy. A teacher who offers choices rather than control, and who acknowledges students' perspectives helps them integrate positive school behaviors into the self. An authoritative teacher introjects directives that may result in students' compliance or defiance, but not integration.

Deci offers the following advice when a teacher has to set limits that students might not like. Teachers can do the following:

- ◆ Prompt students to set their own limits.
- ◆ Avoid controlling language and learn how to handle students' resistance.
- ◆ Help students understand the reasons for limits.
- ◆ Encourage students to determine for themselves why the limits might help them personally.
- ◆ Determine appropriate consequences if limits are not adopted.

- Keep lines of communication open and continuously strive to understand the students' perspective.

And here is one last idea from Robert Brooks (2005):

- Ask student how they want you to remind them when they are not doing their best.

Deci also gives an excellent explanation of the differences between punishment and consequences. He explains that consequences are fundamentally unlike punishment because consequences are about teaching responsibility. For instance, the best gift a teacher can give her students is the understanding that life is full of choices each of which bears certain inevitable consequences. Another gift a teacher gives can be helping students set class goals. He suggests the following:

- Involve everyone in the process.
- Avoid evaluating people or ideas.
- Look at all issues as problems that can be solved.

In terms of our current era of accountability, Deci suggests that teachers who feel pressure to achieve high test scores may become too controlling. Teachers who adopt the role of enforcer of high standards can lose sight of the students' best interests. They could be unsuccessful if they do not keep the idea of the role of intrinsic motivation in mind. It is easy to allow self-motivated students free reign, but harder to deal with students who constantly seem to make bad choices. Also, a student must be sincerely interested in understanding why she is behaving as she is and must stop blaming others for the problem behavior. The student must be ready to choose a different behavior.

(2) What Do Students Say Motivates Them?

Ronald W. Luce explains, in "Motivating the Unmotivated" (1990), that teachers often absolve themselves of using strategies that engage students in learning, and they simply blame the students for not being motivated to learn the material. Although this article is about teaching college students, these ideas have relevance for the KB12 teacher also. Luce says that many students do not actually know *how* to learn and that it is the teacher's job to teach them not only content, but also *how to learn* that content. He says that most students want to learn because they know that education is the key to a better life. Too many teachers, however, do not know how to reach their students and some do not try because they blame their students for not being motivated. Luce asked his students in his college classes what they wanted from the college experience and they replied the following (p. 2):

◆ They want to have their specific needs met. They do not want to be viewed as just one of the crowd of students, but as individuals with talents and abilities that should be respected and nurtured.

◆ They want teachers who care about them and do not see them as merely potential positive or negative test scores.

◆ "They want to be challenged, not decimated."

◆ They want an advocate who understands their learning styles and who gives them an opportunity to use their strengths to accomplish assignments and to show what they know.

◆ They want teachers who talk on their level, who joke with them, and who let them learn in groups with their peers.

◆ They like clear, complete explanations with short examples of difficult information and opportunities to get their questions answered.

Luce says if teachers have the attitude "sit down, shut up, and listen so that you can memorize facts to dump onto a test sheet" they will not do much to motivate students. Luce blames most motivation issues on the depersonalization of the traditional classroom.

(3) Teaching Styles
That Create Motivation Issues

Unfortunately, sometimes the teacher's presentation style creates a motivation issue. In 1916, John Dewey said the following: "Why is it, in spite of the fact that teaching by pouring in learning by a passive absorption, are universally condemned, that they are still so entrenched in practice? That education is not an affair of 'telling' or being told, but an active and constructive process." In addition, Dewey explained that it is the job of a school to educate the young to be productive members of a democratic society, but teachers often lose sight of that purpose and schools can become irrelevant and uninteresting to the young. He says further, that the many formal skills students must learn, such as reading, writing, and mathematics, must be balanced with relevancy so that students will see the reasons to learn them. It is hard to believe that the same unproductive and boring teaching practices are still around 89 years later, and they are not just still around, they dominate classroom practices.

John I. Goodlad (2004) and his team of researchers conducted one of the largest research projects having to do with schools. His findings support the evaluation by Dewey that poor teaching methods dominate education, which is a sad commentary on how entrenched poor teaching practices are in our schools.

Karen D. Wood also comments on encouraging teachers to develop practices that are more engaging. In her helpful book *Practical Strategies for Improving Instruction* (1994), she offers alternatives to five specific teaching practices that *do not* motivate many learners and that are still entrenched in our schools (pp.1B5). Those practices and her suggestions are summarized in the accompanying table, "Improving Instruction."

Improving Instruction

Customary Practice	Better Ideas
Lecturing, telling, mentioning; assigning work rather than teaching.	Cooperative and collaborative learning groups; teachers thinking aloud with students.
Assigning dictionary work to find word meanings. Asking students to read chapters and answer questions without doing the following: preparing them to read, stating a clear purpose for reading, or having a discussion after reading.	Using meaningful vocabulary development strategies and teaching students to read strategically.
Having a single assignment for all students; using the textbook, worksheets, and workbooks too much.	Using a variety of print and nonprint resources, study guides, and peer reading and retelling.
Skill and drill, literal-level thinking, seat work, and memorization.	Active learning, experiential activities, promoting higher order thinking skill development.
Recalling facts and literal-level questioning.	Asking high level questions, using small-group problem-solving strategies, using statements as opposed to questions (i.e., big ideas).

(4) Teaching Practices That Are Best in Terms of Motivation.

As with discipline issues, there is disagreement among professionals about which practices are most engaging, and therefore less likely to create motivation issues for students. I will explain two major theory debates: Constructivism versus Objectivism and Differentiation versus One Plan Fits All. Next, I will help you determine which theory is most clearly aligned with the BESST Criterion.

Constructivism Versus Objectivism

As teachers develop their presentation styles, they may choose between being a constructivist or an objectivist as indicated in the accompanying table.

Objectivism	Constructivism
The teacher understands information, skills, and so on, and imparts knowledge to the students. (See AThe Objectivist Model, which follows.) This is a linear, power- over model.	Students encounter information and a need for skills in order to make meaning and/or create solutions with coaching or facilitation from the teacher. This is a circular, collaborative model.

Objectivism is supported by those who view direct instruction as the best method for teaching students skills and information. This method promotes the idea that unless information flows from the teacher, the students cannot learn. This idea goes along with the emphasis on covering a designated amount of information so that students will have access to the knowledge and skills they need to succeed on standardized tests. It also coincides with discipline methods that place strong control in the hands of the teacher. Objectivism is strongly promoted in many literacy programs that are scripted and require choral or demand responses from students.

Parker Palmer (1998) has graphically represented the concept of the *objectivist* versus the *community of truth* models. (See "Objectivist Model" and "Community of Truth," which follow.) In his conceptualization of the objectivist model, truth flows to the expert (or teacher) who then disseminates it to the amateurs (or students). Amateurs cannot access truth directly, but need the intervention of the expert. Although most people believe that we all have access to information (or the truth) and might believe that this model is not the best way to teach students, many teachers make teaching decisions that reflect this model. For instance, many teachers plan instruction based on the belief that if they do not explain something to their students, the students will not get it.

Objectivist Model

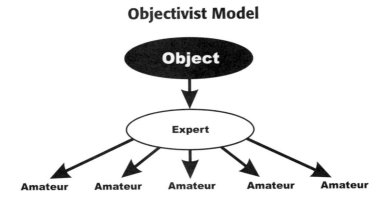

Palmer's community of truth model assumes that the subject, which is open for discussion, is central to learning. This model is not linear as is the objectivist model; instead, it is circular and always moving and changing.

Community of Truth

The community of truth model can easily be interpreted as a constructivist model.

Many teachers may believe that students should construct meaning and learn by struggling with information; however, when it comes to reality in this age of accountability, many of them feel there is simply *not time* to allow students to construct their own learning in real-world situations or simulations. Many would say teachers must base instruction on a constructivist model if they want learning to occur at all. For example, who is wasting time, the teacher who tells students information that they promptly forget (some call this a "core dump"), or the teacher who plans instruction that allows time for students' natural curiosity and motivation to drive them toward real learning?

Differentiation Versus One Plan Fits All

Another opposing view in curriculum design is differentiation of instruction versus the one-plan-fits-all six-step lesson plan. The major differences are indicated in the accompanying table.

Differentiation	One Plan Fits All
Tailoring instructional content, product, or process to meet the needs of students according to their readiness, learning styles, and interests.	Planning instruction for all students using a six-step lesson plan, such as the following: warm-up, review, instruction, guided practice, independent practice, review. Teachers teach to the top or middle of the class readiness levels. Teacher plans based on his/her own interests and learning styles.

Although using one plan for all students may be easier for the teacher, it may not be helpful for all students. It is unlikely that one plan will address all needs of the students in the room. The six-step lesson plan is the traditional method that most districts embrace as best practice. Administrators inform teachers that they will be evaluated on this or a similar plan. They encourage teachers to engage all learners, review, present, practice, and review again. While this six-step plan can accommodate differentiation, most districts do not evaluate teachers on their abilities to differentiate for all learners. They especially do not expect beginning teachers to be able to differentiate. Differentiation is nearly impossible for teachers who believe students cannot learn unless they *tell* them information. While some textbooks in some content areas offer suggestions for adapting lessons for students with differing levels of readiness, they seldom suggest differentiation for learning styles or interests.

Good differentiation meets the needs of all students; therefore, it is inherently motivating. For instance, if teachers make it a priority to learn about students' abilities, learning styles, and interests, they will not usually have to plead with students to learn. See my *Handbook on Differentiating Instruction in Middle and High School* (Northey, 2005) for a full discussion of methods of differentiating instruction.

Teachers working with students who are unmotivated, might look to the process of differentiation to solve the problem. Barring family or psychological issues, differentiation along with noncontrolling classroom management may best address students' motivation.

(5) Evaluating Opposing Views Based on the BESST Criterion = Value Added

Once again, we see opposing views when it comes to the challenge of unmotivated students. I evaluate these views based on the BESST Criterion.

BESST Criterion = Value Added

Brain-Based	Ethical	Standards	Systems Theory
In an environment where students' goals are aligned with classroom experiences, the brain motivates itself to learn without being bribed by rewards or threatened by punishment.	All people (including children) are created equal with equal rights to freedom, happiness, and the Golden Rule.	Extensive skills and knowledge help teachers provide a positive learning environment.	Having an awareness of the interactions that make up an environment helps teachers respectfully and strategically plan their actions.

- ♦ *Brain-Based:* Brain-based research supports constructivism and differentiation because it says that the brain seeks its own rewards, craves complexity, and creates its own meaning. It is well documented that students do not respond well to one-size-fits-all lecture; however, many educators believe that direct instruction, a form of objectivism, is superior to constructivism. They claim their programs are differentiated because they are leveled to match the readiness needs of students. Advocates of direct instruction believe their programs are helpful because they believe the following: that the affect is irrelevant in learning, that a skilled instructor can lead the class toward learning by using a well-crafted choral response program that focuses all students, and that a competitive reward system will motivate student participation. They feel that research supports these conclusions.

◆ *Ethics:* Objectivism and one-size-fits-all lesson plans do not fit well with collaboration. They both assume that the teacher's knowledge and skill are more important than the students' abilities or needs. They both take the view that the teacher is superior to the students. Even though adults do have more life experiences than their students and should have more knowledge of their subject, they should not see themselves as more valuable as people than their students. This devaluing of students can cause disrespect and lower levels of ethical behavior, such as acting as if might makes right or being good to comply with an authority figure.

◆ *Standards:* The standards do not rule out one-size-fits all lesson plans or objectivism; however, they do insist that instruction be aligned with students' needs and that teachers should have significant knowledge and skills to engage all learners. The more knowledge teachers have, the less they have to rely on one-size-fits all lecture to teach students. The more they know, the more they can trust students to construct their own meaning. It takes great skill to allow students to construct their own meaning and to differentiate instruction to meet all students' needs. That master teachers have great skill in engaging students to learn is certainly a standard. Theoretically, a master teacher should be able to create an atmosphere for learning that motivates any student.

◆ *Systems Theory:* With systems thinking in mind, teachers can consider the dynamics of the class and the school and district in which the class exists. Teachers should consider the family systems that students come from. Some schools require teachers to use scripted lessons or direct instruction programs. If a required program does not motivate a student, a skilled teacher might adjust that program to meet students' needs or give the student an alternative assignment. If the teacher takes the side of the students and asks them if they like the program, she might be able to make it useful to her students.

◆ *= Value Added:* Constructivism and differentiation add value to students' lives. With these models, students motivate themselves and discover what they value, rather than what an authority says they have to value. Students learn that they can access learning from their own questions and realize they are not dependent on the expert to make sense of the world for them.

Constructivism and differentiation also add value to the lives of teachers who can share in the joys of learning that they see in the faces of their students who are discovering answers to their important questions. A teacher can be delighted when a student asks a question and truly cares to know the answer. Or the teacher can ask a question and know the students care about the answer.

(6) Other Issues Related to Student Motivation—Challenges and Solutions

Diversity

Nearly a century ago, John Dewey (1916) said, "The intermingling in the school of youth of different races, differing religions, and unlike customs creates for all a new and broader environment" (p. 21). This statement makes it clear that Dewey promoted diversity as advantageous to our educational process. Unfortunately, many are grossly uninformed about other cultures, and worst of all, many are unaware that they are uninformed; they often create hardships for others because of their lack of understanding and insensitivity.

According to Wlodkowski and Ginsberg (1995), one way to motivate students is for districts or teachers to design a curriculum that responds to cultural diversity. The best programs include the following four features: includes all learners, improves attitudes toward learning, supports students' construction of meaning, and promotes students' achievement. Ginsberg (2004) suggests that teachers make a strong commitment to planning curriculum that includes the above four elements and that they avoid inconsistencies such as promoting cooperative learning but then making individuals' assessment competitive. Her book *Motivation Matters* suggests a step-by-step method to promote change in order to improve students' motivation.

Optimal Life Experiences

Beyond motivating students to learn, there are ways to make the learning experience optimal. Mihaly Csikszentmihalyi (1990) researched various optimal life experiences and proposed the concept of *flow*. Csikszentmihalyi discovered that when people explain their most positive activities they usually include one or more of the following:

♦ They feel they can complete the task.

♦ They can concentrate on what they are doing.

♦ They can concentrate because the goals are clear and the feedback immediate.

◆ The concentration on the activity makes them forget their worries and concerns of daily life.

◆ They feel a sense of control over their actions.

◆ They feel a loss of concern about the self, and yet more in tune with the self.

◆ Their sense of time is either much longer or much shorter than in reality.

Csikszentmihalyi says that there is a "golden ratio," a balance between challenges and skills when "enjoyment appears at the boundary between boredom and anxiety, when the challenges are just balanced with the person's capacity to act" (p. 52). The chart "Flow," adapted here from his book (p. 78), shows that when one is in the state of flow, his skills improve as he meets his challenges.

Flow

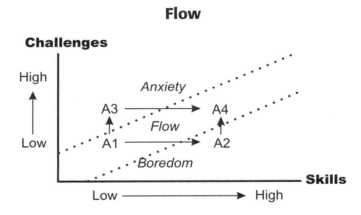

In the chart "Flow," the two most important aspects of an experience, challenge (anxiety) and skills (boredom), are located on opposite axes of the diagram. The A represents a person (Alex) who is learning to play a sport at four points in time (A1, A2, A3, A4). At A1, Alex is just learning to play the sport so that his skill level is low, but he can enjoy the sport because as a beginner he is not bored with his lack of skill nor will he ask too much of his abilities so that he becomes anxious. As he continues in time to play the sport, he will become bored (A2) if he does not challenge himself to develop more skills, and he will become anxious (A3) if he challenges himself too much. At A2, he will be bored with his novice abilities if he does not challenge himself and anxious if he gets into a situation for which he is not prepared. At A3, Alex may have made himself anxious because he has signed up for a tournament before he is ready to compete. At A4, he has challenged himself and mastered the skills at a higher level. Alex will stay in a state of flow as long as he challenges himself when he becomes bored but does not challenge himself unreasonably beyond his capacities so that he becomes anxious.

As teachers plan lessons, they could keep in mind the concept of flow. They plan lessons that reflect the golden ratio that balances the anxiety about doing a challenging task with the boredom of doing an oversimplified task. If teachers plan lessons that help students achieve this balance, students will be intrinsically motivated to move forward in skills and self-confidence.

Breaking Out

In his book *The Breakout Principal* (2003), Dr. Herbert Benson, who also defined the relaxation response, describes a method for problem solving that takes a person to a high level of creativity and productivity. Benson refers to a pattern related to our response to stress, a pattern similar to Csikszentmihalyi's concept of flow. This pattern, described in 1908 by Yerkes and Dodson, is called the Yerkes-Dodson Law. See the following "Stress-Performance Curve" to learn how it works (Benson, p. 32).

Stress-Performance Curve

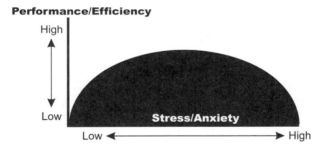

As we begin to work on a problem our energy needs to be high, and it may actually be beneficial to encounter some amounts of stress if we want to complete the entire task; however, if we continue experiencing anxiety about the task for a prolonged period, the stress will eventually overwhelm us and greatly reduce our ability to perform successfully.

In light of this relationship, Benson suggests that we should struggle with an issue but then back away from it and focus on other activities that take our minds off of our problem. (In his book, he includes a wonderful list of suggested activities, such as taking a long walk, meditating, and reading for pleasure.) Benson states that following this interruption in the struggles, we might suddenly see a clear solution to the problem, and thus move forward happily and fulfilled. Teachers might use this pattern themselves when they are planning ways to solve teaching problems; they might also teach students to use it. The process is outlined in "Breakout Pattern," which follows (Benson, p. 20):

Breakout Pattern

Breakout/peak experience

Struggle

Release

New normal state;
Improved mind-body patterns
Brain

Brain-Brain Based Research

Brain-based researcher Eric Jensen, in his book *Teaching with the Brain in Mind* (1998), explains that we now have actual evidence from brain studies to substantiate the concepts that psychologists like Maslow, Yerkes, and Dodson conceptualized from observing people's behavior many years ago. In addition to proving the ideas of people like John Dewey, Mihaly Csikszentmihalyi, Edward Deci, and many others, Jensen explains several critical pieces of information that have a direct relationship to the idea of motivating students to learn. One of the most interesting ideas is that the brain has its own reward system.

As mentioned in Chapter 1, brain-based research adds to our knowledge of what motivates students. Please review the pages in Chapter 1 that describe how a teacher might design her classroom with the brain in mind. I highly recommend teachers learn all they can about how the brain works to help students learn. New ideas come to our attention constantly and we should make sure we are aligning teaching with our students' potential for learning.

(7) Using the Five Pause-Point System of Decision Making With a Student Motivation Issue

Here is an example of how I used this model to plan and implement a poetry unit in a class I taught some time ago. I had to make a plan of what to do *after* our state standardized tests were over. I thought about asking students to do a poetry project, and I began the process:

P1CPlanning an Action:

1. Would I need to use bribery or punishment and were my goals aligned with students' goals?

   I would not need to bribe students to participate because most of them were interested in poetry, at least in terms of pop culture's song lyrics. I would not need to use punishment for the same reason.

2. Would my poetry project hurt anyone or help anyone?

   I could show my students that the song lyrics they loved to print from the computer and that reflect their cultural system are poems that they could share and analyze as an enjoyable process. I also knew my students love to be video taped; therefore, I planned for them to share the poems in a presentation that I would tape. In terms of not hurting anyone, I would not insist that someone be taped if it made him feel uncomfortable. In order to be respectful of individuals by not imposing my will, I also asked students to choose other authors' poems or write their own poems. As far as not hurting myself, I knew I could relax and enjoy this unit because I love poetry and I could enjoy the entire process.

3. Would I demonstrate skills and knowledge?

   I knew all of my students had weaknesses in analyzing poetry, so that just getting them to see some connections between their songs and poetry analyzing skills would help them a great deal. I used their natural interests to greatly improve their knowledge of poetry. Giving choices, showing connections between natural interests and academics, and being sensitive to individual preferences demonstrated knowledge of my students and skills in developing and implementing and engaging lesson.

4. Was I being sensitive to the system?

   This lesson would show awareness of the cultural system within which these students functioned. By denying the effect of these pop culture heroes on my students, I would have missed an opportunity to use that interest as an academic learning opportunity. For instance, seeing the connection between pop culture songs and the concept of poetry could improve students' interest in poetry and decrease resistance toward analyzing it. Using pop culture interests to engage students in learning poetry elements improves thinking skills and reading comprehension skills. Giving choices motivates students to learn more about poetry.

   In terms of the effect of the larger system: I knew that two other teachers had also recently completed poetry projects. I got a copy of one of them and noticed that it was far more complicated and demanding than the one I was planning. I thought my project would help my students who were less academically motivated see the joy of poetry rather than the challenge of it.

P2CImplementation/Observation: I implemented the poetry plan, but I had mixed results. Some of the students complained that they had just completed a poetry project in their Language Arts classes and they were burned-out on poetry. They did not hurry to begin the project. Other students seemed enthusiastic about doing the project and jumped right in with decorating the cover of their poetry project booklet.

P3: Reflection:

1. Were my goals aligned with students' goals so that I did not need bribery or punishment?

    I felt tempted to bribe or threaten those students who were burned out on poetry; however, I resisted that temptation and encouraged them to come up with an alternative plan.

2. Did my plan hurt anyone or help anyone?

    I feel I may have inadvertently hurt some students because even though I knew my students needed more practice in analyzing poetry, some of them were tired of it. I realized I had not considered the effect of another class on my plans. I also helped some students because some of them seemed to see the difference between my project and the one they did in Language Arts. They saw a way to use what they learned in their Language Arts classes to help them succeed on our poetry project. This project seemed different enough from the other project that I was able to show the resistant students that it was fun and educational.

3. Did I demonstrate knowledge and skill to create a positive learning environment?

    The project demonstrated thorough knowledge of poetry and why we analyze it: not merely as an academic exercise but also to see how an author's use of techniques deepens our understanding and enjoyment of a poem and of life. It also showed skill in adapting to the special needs and interests of students in order to allow them the choices that kept them engaged and constructing their own meaning.

4. Did I have awareness of the effect on the system?

    This project allowed the classroom system to hum with the self-directed activity of highly engaged students. Within the school as a whole, it kept my students out of the office during a time (the last days of school) in which they were more vulnerable to getting into trouble.

P4CRevision: I continued with the project, but found a way to meet the needs of students who were burned out on poetry. I let them choose an alternate project if they were truly tired of thinking about poetry. I made sure they were also challenged to learn something, but did not fight their resistance to my idea. I collaborated with my colleagues to get their ideas about how to reach the students who seemed burned out on poetry.

P5CAction With More KnowledgeCValue Added: I continued to plan, implement, observe, reflect, and revise my actions in terms of this project until the video-taped sharing activity, which was a glowing success. Students were thrilled to see themselves on the television screen and we watched the tape several times. I have added value to my students' lives by facilitating their motivation to see the relevance of poetry to improve their lives. I have also added value to my teaching ability because I used skills and knowledge to improve the likelihood that students will relate poetry to their own lives and will be more willing to create their own poetry as a means of positive self-expression.

(8) Suggestions for Dealing With Your Own School System

Think aboutY

♦ Yourself

- Make sure you have a solid understanding of what motivates people (students and adults) within each of their systems (classroom, school, family).

- Observe carefully the effect of giving people choices and siding with them on issues that the larger system imposes or that are necessary for a smooth-running class or school.

- Examine your actions to make sure you are using recognition and consequences rather than bribery and punishment. There is a fine line between the two approaches, and it may take practice, journaling, and/or an informed colleague to keep you honest about using the better stance.

- Use your role as the executive in the classroom to facilitate self-motivation and autonomy.

- Do not give mixed messages to students about your belief system; for instance, do not lose your temper and resort to using punishment to get revenge.

- Watch your language; semantics are everything.

◆ Students

- Observe the effect of choices on them. Do not let them make you choose for them. Help them understand that choosing is a sign of maturity and true self-esteem.

- Have classroom meetings to show them the power of discussion.

- Help them see that they do not need external rewards in order to learn.

◆ Parents

- Model choices for parents and help them see how these choices motivate students.

- Give parents choices for how you deal with their child.

- Enter a family system with great respect and honor. Treat all kinds of parents as your partners. Join with them and be "on their side" no matter what. See them as doing the best they can for their child not as someone who is trying to get you fired. (Even though that might be their bottom line; unless you have done something that would be grounds for getting fired, you are safe.)

◆ Administrators and Other Colleagues

- Recognizing that motivation is intrinsic, do not force your ideas on anyone.

- Use modeling and reporting good results to speak for the benefits of your system of dealing with students.

- Be prepared to adjust based on the larger system's stance. Do not get into arguments with others or go against a team or school decision to use a reward or punishment system. Remember that systems resist change and you must not jeopardize your career to fight for what you think is right. You might, however, respectfully state your ideas and do what you can to show the larger system how well your ideas work within your sphere of influence.

◆ District and Community

- Become a voice for better ways to motivate students.

- Advocate for professional development that would help teachers see the benefits of enlightened teaching practices that address motivation issues.

Summary

When considering the issue of unmotivated students within the classroom, within the school, within the family, and within the district, we may consider that all systems have for years functioned under the premise that rewards and punishments are the way to discipline and motivate students, and that if a teacher knows how to control the variables, he or she will be able to discipline and motivate. Based on better ideas from the past and new findings from empirical research, this is simply not the case.

There is a major split in the way teachers address students' motivation. Perhaps because of years of objectivist role models and perhaps simply due to arrogance, many teachers are still tied to the idea that if they do not directly instruct students on skills and content, the students will not learn it. Despite all the research that disproves any benefits of using rewards and punishment to motivate students' behavior, these outmoded methods remain entrenched in our schools. It may seem counterintuitive to stop the use of these outmoded methods. However, with the emergence of standards and with more research about the negative effects of bribery, punishment, and one-size-fits-all objectivist teaching practices, educators will gradually shift toward better practices, such as giving students a variety of interesting choices about learning content or skills.

4

Dealing With Underinvolved or Adversarial Parents

What Are the Challenges?

After discipline issues, one of the most disturbing challenges for teachers is dealing with those parents who are underinvolved with the school or adversarial toward them and/or toward administrators. For instance, it is most disturbing when a school holds an important schoolwide meeting and only a handful of parents attend. It is also disturbing when a teacher calls parents for assistance with their child's behavior, and the parents blame the teacher for the problem. If a parent says to the school "*my child* is not the problem, *you* are" or if a parent says, "my child is not *my* problem, he/she is *your* problem," then everyone suffers.

Research (Henderson & Berla, 1981, 1995) supports the view that the most accurate predictor of student achievement in school is not social status or income; it is parent involvement. However, if this is so, why do so many schools have poor parent involvement and negative parent-teacher relationships? In this chapter, I provide information on the following topics: (1) How role perspectives affect how parents and teachers get along, (2) What constitutes a good parent-teacher relationship, (3) Evaluation of opposing views based on the BESST Criterion, (4) Using the five pause-point decision-making process with a problem parent, (5) The effect of poverty on parent-teacher relationships. (6) Why we have problem parents, (7) Standards for involving parents, (8) Strategies for getting parents more involved in your school, (9) What to do about adversarial parents, and (10) Suggestions for dealing with your own school system.

(1) How Role Perspectives Affect How Parents and Teachers Get Along

Carol Keyes says there are three factors that affect positive relationships between parents and teachers: (1) the degree with which the culture and values of the parents match the teachers' culture and values, (2) the social system forces that affect the family and the school, and (3) how teachers and families view their roles in relation to each other. Keyes (n.d.) states that today's teachers are less likely to share the culture and values of the students than in the past when teachers tended to be more like their students and may have even lived in the same neighborhood with their students. Now teachers' socioeconomic class, race, and ethnic group are usually quite different from the students they teach. This difference is evident in social interaction style, language system, and values.

Another way to think about causes of conflict is, according to Keyes, confusion over role perceptions. See "Parent Teacher Roles." Among the parents you work with, which of these perspectives do they take? Which perspective do you take?

Parent Teacher Roles

Professional Distance	Extended Family
A good parent-teacher relationship is one in which there is an effective separation of roles between school and home. Teachers and parents are respectful but maintain a social distance. The family complies with the expectations of the school, and the school makes no unrealistic demands on the family (Henry, 1996; Epstein, 1995; Powell, 1989; Lortie, 1975).	A good parent-teacher relationship is one in which the school functions as an extended family. This is an open system where all the adults come together for the benefit of the child (Powell, 1989; Galinsky, 1988; Taylor, 1968).

In summary, the best parent-teacher relationships are based on mutual trust and respect, and there are several ways to minimize conflict and help develop relationships that are more positive. Unfortunately, sometimes parent-teacher relationships are conflict-free because neither the parents nor the teacher care enough to bother fighting for the needs of the child (Keyes, n.d.).

(2) What Constitutes a Good Parent-Teacher Relationship?

According to Carol Keyes (n.d.), most teachers want to have good relationships with the parents of the students they teach. And yet how do we decide what exactly constitutes a *good* parent-teacher relationship? She describes a *spectrum of perspectives on relationships,* shown here in "Parent-Teacher Relationship Spectrum."

Parent-Teacher Relationship Spectrum

Parent's Belief System (How they view their roles)[1]		
Parent focused: Parents believe they have the primary responsibility for their child's education.	*Teacher focused:* Parents believe the teachers have primary responsibility for their child's education.	*Partnership focused:* Parents believe the teachers and parents working together have responsibility for their child's education.
Teacher's Belief System (How they view their roles)		
Parent focused: This idea came from the "parent cooperative movement." Parents and teachers worked side-by-side and parents took teaching roles. Teachers believe parent volunteers can be extremely useful at more than just tutoring.	*Teacher focused:* Teachers believe in a separation between school and home. This belief most prevalent in high school.	*Partnership focused:* This is a more recent perspective as teachers have learned how important parent involvement can be for students' achievement.
1 Keyes cites Reed, Jones, Walker, and Hoover-Dempsey (2000) when outlining these parental beliefs.		

(3) Evaluation of Opposing Views Based on the BESST Criterion = Value Added

The opposing views that we should evaluate are between those who believe parents should keep a professional distance and those who believe parents should be part of the school family. What does the BESST Criterion = Value Added say about these opposing views?

BESST Criterion = Value Added

Brain-Based	Ethical	Standards	Systems Theory
In an environment where students' goals are aligned with classroom experiences, the brain motivates itself to learn without being bribed by rewards or threatened by punishment.	All people (including children) are created equal with equal rights to freedom, happiness, and the Golden Rule.	Extensive skills and knowledge help teachers provide a positive learning environment.	Having an awareness of the interactions that make up an environment helps teachers respectfully and strategically plan their actions.

- ♦ *Brain-Based:* Brain-based research supports the idea that feelings assist learning. If the parents do not connect with the school, then it is likely that the child won't either. Therefore, professional distance seems less supported by brain-based research than does the extended family model. For instance, as the parent's emotionally support the school, so will their child improve in his ability to attach to the teachers and the school program.

- ♦ *Ethics:* If parents are allowed to share in the responsibility of the school, they will feel more involved, and therefore, their children may feel more responsible for their school. Respecting and valuing diverse families whose children you teach is easier to do if you see their parents as part of a school family. It may be harder to show that respect and valuing if you keep your families at a professional distance. Professional distance allows for judgmental behaviors and power struggles to flourish.

- ♦ *Standards:* All of the standards insist that parents form partnerships with teachers and other school personnel. These partnerships could be business partnerships that reflect professional distance, but a family model partnership seems more supported by the standards when it comes to the well-being of the child. In the difficult case of a challenging family, teachers who have the skills and knowledge to develop a close and trusting relationship with these families are often more successful than those who maintain professional distance.

◆ *Systems Theory:* Systems theory supports open communication, which does not seem to support professional distance. Knowledge of the impact of each child's family on the classroom supports the idea that teachers might connect with the families of their students as closely as time and personalities will allow.

◆ = *Value Added:* Having close relationships with students' families adds value to the lives of students. When the adults are aligned in their goals for helping children, children can be assured that they are being taught by those who know children and care about them.

(4) Using the Five Pause-Point System of Decision Making With a Problem Parent

Some time ago, two of my students got into an argument that became physical. I had my back turned as they were pushing each other; therefore, I could not be a witness and each child was saying the other did something that they both denied doing. I knew that both students' fathers were not always complimentary of the teachers at our school; therefore, I needed to plan carefully what to do.

P1—Planning an action: I needed to plan how I could keep those fathers on my side and get some kind of resolution for the students' use of physical aggression.

1. Would my plan need bribery or punishment? Was it aligned with students' and parents' goals?

   In the case of dealing with parents, I knew I could not bribe them to agree with me or punish them by punishing their child. That is, I could not use those techniques if I wanted them to be my partners in dealing with the issue. I wanted to align my goals with the needs of the students and their parents. I did not have a goal to have my way regardless of their needs.

2. Would I hurt any one or help anyone?

   I did not want to hurt either child by having their fathers turn against me; therefore, I had to be very careful not to appear unconcerned or unresponsive to their needs to have their children protected from harm. However, I did not want either child to continue to argue, especially to the point where they might take physical actions against each other.

3. Would my plan show knowledge and skill to create a positive environment?

   I needed to have knowledge of how to deal with angry parents and skill in keeping my own emotions under control so that I could maintain objectivity and respectfulness at all times. Knowing that I would not have to take a stand or get my way about the problem, relieved me of the tension that fighting for your way can cause. In other words, knowing how to be a listener and facilitator rather than an enforcer would help me create a positive environment for negotiating a win-win solution.

4. Would my plan show awareness to the system it affects?

   Knowledge of systemic intervention helped me know that siding with each of the fathers would help me align with their needs and would make the process of getting the students to solve their issues much easier. It would also help me build a partnership with these men, who had dealt with teachers who may not have been as collaborative as I knew how to be. (Their negative attitudes about dealing with teachers came from somewhere.)

5. What would I do?

   I would contact each father by telephone and find out his concerns. I would offer to collaborate with each parent so that we could determine what the best plan of action might be.

P2—Implementation/Observation: I called each of the fathers and had wonderful conversations with each of them. They wanted their children to be able to talk about their problem with a caring adult facilitator, and they wanted to know if the issues were resolved. Allowing these fathers to suggest the method of dealing with the issue worked beautifully. I felt like I made two friends rather than two enemies because I was willing and able to collaborate rather than dictate.

P3—Reflection:

1. Did I need bribery or punishment? Were my goals aligned with parents' and students' goals?

   I did not need to bribe anyone with idle promises or threats because my actions were aligned with students' and parents' goals.

2. Did I hurt anyone or help anyone?

   Both students calmed down because the adults were behaving calmly and modeling cooperation. The attitudes exhibited by the fathers were much more positive, so that they seemed to benefit from the interactions and regain faith in our school.

3. Did I demonstrate knowledge and skills to create a positive environment?

   I was able to use my knowledge of negotiating with parents and the skill of staying objective to keep the situation from escalating. Developing a partnership with their parents helped create an environment in which students resolved their issue more easily.

4. Did I show awareness of the system I affected?

   The impact on the system was that no further aggression or violence occurred and two parents developed closer relationships with the school.

5. What should I do?

   Be glad that everyone is happy with the results and relax knowing it could have been a horrible situation if it had been mishandled.

P4—Revision: Based on my reflection, I did not need to revise my actions.

P5—Action With More Knowledge—Value Added: I gained two allies that I could call upon to support the school and our class. I continued to contact these fathers if any problems came up. These fathers became my partners rather than my adversaries. I added value to my skills as a negotiator who knows how to promote win-win solutions. The parents and students learned to work with the school to resolve conflict appropriately.

(5) The Effect of Poverty on Parent-Teacher Relationships

Poverty can cause problems for parent-teacher relationships. Research shows that schools with high numbers of students of poverty and high levels of minority students have fewer incidents of positive parent involvement (Epstein, 1995; National Center for Education Statistics, 1998). It is important to understand as much as possible about the effects of poverty on parent-teacher relationships. In her book *A Framework for Understanding Poverty* (2001), Ruby Payne explains the differences in culture and values that result from poverty. The following is a list of key points to remember when thinking about poor families (pp. 10–11):

◆ Poverty is relative. If everyone around you has similar circumstances, the notion is vague.

♦ Poverty occurs in all races and in all countries. The idea of a middle class is a relatively recent phenomenon.

♦ Economic class is a continuum, not a clear-cut distinction.

♦ Distinguish between generational poverty and situational poverty. Generational poverty is poverty that has existed for at least two generations. Situational poverty is shorter and based on an incident (death, illness, divorce).

♦ Just because poverty presents certain patterns does not mean that there are no exceptions to those patterns.

♦ An individual brings with him the hidden rules of the class in which he was reared. Even though the income may increase, certain patterns of thought, social interactions, and so on remain.

♦ Schools and businesses operate from middle-class norms and use the hidden rules of the middle class. These norms and hidden rules are not taught in schools and businesses.

♦ For impoverished students to be successful in school, we teachers must counteract these hidden rules with rules that will make these students successful at school and at work.

♦ We can neither excuse students nor scold them for not knowing the rules of middle class; as educators we must teach them and provide support, insistence, and expectations.

♦ To move from poverty to middle class or middle class to wealth, an individual must give up relationships for achievement (at least for some period of time).

Most teachers did not come from poverty; therefore, their culture and values may not match with those of the parents of these students. This cultural mismatch could cause major challenges to teachers and parents developing positive relationships. For instance, most teachers do not understand the hidden rules of poverty, and they may not know how to communicate effectively with parents who speak another language; therefore, they may look down on those who have less education than they do, and they may have difficulty truly accepting child-rearing practices that they cannot fully understand. Unfortunately, although some teachers may give lip service to diversity, in actuality, they may be unable to communicate trust and respect to those families who are diverse in terms of culture.

What follows are some ideas about how teachers and parents might work together for the benefits of the children.

(6) Why We Have Problem Parents

Other perspectives concerning why parents and teachers have problems working together come from Elaine K. McEwan, who has written a useful book on this subject, *How to Deal With Parents Who Are Angry, Troubled, Afraid, or Just Plain Crazy* (1998). Although her main audience is administrators, teachers can also learn a great deal from this book, which is a product of research and her own experiences. McEwan provides excellent detail concerning why parents are harder to work with now than they were in the past. McEwan says that today's challenging parents can have any of the following characteristics:

- ♦ They are less respectful of authority. (Just like their children.)
- ♦ They are more educated and consumer oriented.
- ♦ They can be cynical and distrustful.
- ♦ Some are activists.
- ♦ Some totally reject public school and use alternative methods to educate their children (such as home schooling, charter schools).
- ♦ They are under more stress and sometimes feel guilty about their role as parents.
- ♦ They are worried that schools will fail to help their children achieve in today's competitive society.

She then explains why parents are angry, troubled, afraid, or crazy. She says that many parents are angry with educators for the following reasons:

- ♦ Educators do not communicate enough with parents.
- ♦ Principals often back teachers without knowing the whole story.
- ♦ Educators break promises and put parents off.
- ♦ Educators overreact to students' behavior.
- ♦ Educators make assumptions and stereotype parents.
- ♦ Educators become defensive when parents complain.
- ♦ Educators use educational jargon instead of speaking to parents in language they can understand.
- ♦ Educators use intimidation, blame, control, and power over parents.
- ♦ Educators can be rude and condescending.
- ♦ Educators can be dishonest.
- ♦ Educators can be unwilling to admit to mistakes and apologize.

- ◆ Educators do not give parents credit for understanding their children.
- ◆ Educators can be disrespectful of parents and students.
- ◆ Educators sometimes ask for advice and then ignore it.
- ◆ Educators can be unprofessional.

She also says that parents who are troubled are more difficult to deal with because their issues often revolve around core values: politics, religion, and race. Their issues are as follows:

- ◆ Concern that district and school decisions will not help their children learn what they need to know to be successful.
- ◆ Concern that their child is not being treated as he/she should be treated. (For example: *My* child isn't liked, is unfairly punished, is not guilty, is bored, is failing, is unhappy, is socially unsuccessful, is not given a chance to show what he/she can do best.)
- ◆ Feeling undermined by a conflict of values between what parents think is best and what the school thinks is best.
- ◆ Worries about the effect of a specific curriculum on their child.
- ◆ Concern about the commitment from teachers to do an excellent job for every child.

Next, McEwan says parents who are afraid worry about the following:

- ◆ The general safety of their child.
- ◆ Retaliation from a teacher or administrator if they complain.
- ◆ Being forced to send their child to a low-performing school.
- ◆ Not knowing what the future holds for their children.

Finally, the most difficult group with whom to deal, according to McEwan is the parent who is crazy. She states that these parents fit into the following categories:

- ◆ "School Groupies" (p. 18). These parents want to control the school; some of them are willing to do everything they can to ruin an educator's career if that educator crosses them.
- ◆ Parents who are abusive to educators and to their own children.
- ◆ Parents who are mentally ill, addicted, or otherwise dysfunctional.
- ◆ Parents who chronically complain, whine, and generally make trouble.

Given all of these issues, what can teachers do to improve relationships with parents?

(7) Standards for Involving Parents

An excellent set of standards for parent involvement comes from the work of Joyce L. Epstein (1989, 1995, 1997) of the Center on School, Family, and Community Partnerships at the Johns Hopkins University. She identified six types of parent involvement and the standards that address each type. See "Six Types of Parent Involvement."

Six Types of Parent Involvement

Category	Description
Communicating	Communication between home and school is regular, two-way, and meaningful.
Parenting	Parenting skills are promoted and supported.
Student Learning	Parents play an integral role in assisting student learning.
Volunteering	Parents are welcome in the school, and their support and assistance are sought.
School Decision Making and Advocacy	Parents are full partners in the decisions that affect children and families.
Collaborating With the Community	Community resources are used to strengthen schools, families, and student learning.

Epstein's work (1989, 1997, 1995) is reflected in *Building Successful Partnerships: A Guide for Developing Parent and Family Involvement Programs* (2000), published by the National PTA. Teachers can find extensive discussion of each of Epstein's six standards for parent involvement in this helpful book. For each standard there is the following (and more):

- ♦ An extensive explanation of factors that define the standard
- ♦ Discussion of barriers that inhibit or stifle that standard
- ♦ Research findings
- ♦ Benefits for students, parents, teachers, and administrators who meet the standard
- ♦ Quality tips for successful programs

This book addresses how students, parents, teachers, and administrators can develop beneficial relationships. It also includes information about what teachers, administrators, and PTAs can do to increase parent involvement in order to improve schools.

(8) Strategies for Getting Parents More Involved With Your School[1]

Strategy	Description
Monthly Classroom Bulletins (p. 40)	Send home an interactive notebook, agenda book, or planning book where parents and teachers can ask each other questions and make comments to each other. Write a newsletter informing parents of the news from the class.
"Dear Diary…" (p. 40)	Help students create a journal in which they reflect about their work at school each day. Ask them to share the journal each day with their parents. Ask parents to sign each entry. By the end of the year students have a great record of their learning for the year.
BUDDIES system (pp. 42–43)	BUDDIES stands for Building Unity Despite Diversity in Every Situation. In this program, a survey is sent out in several different languages to find out what languages are spoken in the homes of students and how well each family can read or write English. This information is used to pair families based on language ability. Families help each other deal with school information. A multicultural night caps off the program.
Toy Lending Library (p. 59)	Provide a toy lending library with toys and kits with games and parenting ideas.
Parent University (p. 61)	Offer a series of workshops on parenting skills for various age groups. Have videotapes of sessions available for checkout for families who can not attend sessions.
Celebrate Parents as First Teachers (p.60)	Hold a Parents as First Teachers Night. Talk about how parents can function as children's most important teachers by reading with them at home and helping them with problem solving.

---

1   From National PTA (2000), *Building Successful Partnerships: A Guide for Developing Parent and Family Involvement Programs.*

Strategy	Description
SPAN the Gap (p. 64)	SPAN (Single-Parent Family Advocacy Network) has formed a partnership with the YWCA to provide a range of direct services and advocacy for single-parent families.
TIPS for Student Learning (p. 82)	TIPS (Teachers Involve Parents in Schoolwork) is a strategy whereby teachers make assignments that require students to interact with or get help from their parents. Homework becomes a three-way partnership.
Parent-Student Learning Centers (p. 85)	Parents run a drop-in center where students can go to get help with homework.
Senior Power (p. 101)	Send out surveys to local retirement communities or services to find seniors interested in volunteering in schools.
Create a Yellow Pages of Services (p. 100)	Make a resources book to help match volunteer interests with schools' needs.
Create a "Wall of Fame" (p.101)	Have pictures of volunteers working with students; these pictures can be used to publicize contributions made by volunteers to your school.
Entrepreneur-ship 101 (p. 103)	Partner teachers with adults who have business backgrounds. Create yearlong classroom projects that develop student-run businesses.

I find it interesting that the forward to *Building Successful Partnerships* was written by James Còmer, a pioneer in increasing parent involvement to improve student achievement. In *School Power* (1980), he details how he enticed parents into their children's schools by offering them respect and stipends to improve their abilities to help their children at home. His Comer Schools program has been implemented across the country and shows how using various staff-parent teams and committees can promote school improvement.

(9) What To Do About Adversarial Parents

It is important to get parents more involved with their child's school; however, if parents become involved with the school in order to blame you for a problem, get you in trouble with superiors, or destroy your career, then you may need special strategies to deal with them.

Elaine McEwan (1998) has some excellent suggestions teachers can use to address the challenge of adversarial parents. She says strategies should be based on how one deals with any distressed person; she cautions, however, that these strategies may not be easy for some people and they take practice. If you are a highly emotional person yourself, you made need to practice controlling your emotions in order to stay calm in the face of an angry, troubled, afraid, or crazy parent.

McEwan says there are two "ways to be" (p. 23) if you want to stand a chance of dealing with a challenging parent: Be trustworthy. Have integrity.

- ◆ To be trustworthy, McEwan suggests the following (p. 24):
  - Never talk about people behind their backs. Don't ever verbally assassinate parents or children, even behind the closed doors of a confidential meeting. Your statements might still make their way back to the ears of parents.
  - Don't make promises you can't keep.
  - Do more than you promised you would.
  - Apologize when you're wrong.
  - Confront people with care and respect.
  - Tell the truth in love.
  - Do what you say you're going to do; if you can't do that, let people know what's standing in the way of your following through.
  - Build people up whenever you can.
  - Be punctual.
  - Be thorough and conscientious.
  - Always attack the problem, never the person.
- ◆ Having integrity means the following (p. 24):
  - Be honest with yourself and others.
  - Be consistent in how you behave toward students, parents, other teachers, and administrators.
  - Make decisions based on high standards and values.
  - Do not make decisions based on the three Ps: politics, pressure, and power.
  - Do not let yourself be bullied or bought.
  - Here is an overview of the things McEwan says to do when you are meeting with a parent who is upset with a situation or with you.

- ♦ Shake hands with parents and welcome them to the meeting.
- ♦ Sit eye-to-eye and knee-to-knee if possible.
- ♦ Make a personal connection with parents.
- ♦ Say something positive about the child.
- ♦ Listen carefully to parents' view of the issue. Active listening can take practice and includes the following:
  - Notice the attitudes and feelings.
  - Listen "between the lines."
  - Nod and say "uh huh," or give some other sign of acknowledgment.
  - Take notes.
  - Keep your body language open.
  - Wait until the speaker is completely finished before you speak.
- ♦ Reflect what parents have said by using a technique called *backtracking* or *reflection.* Do not be judgmental. Be like a clear mirror, reflecting parents' messages and reporting what you see the child doing.
- ♦ Keep an open mind.
- ♦ Stay calm and confident that you can deal effectively with the issues.
- ♦ Have a time limit. (Parents will take all the time you allow them to take.)
- ♦ Apologize if you were wrong.

  Here is a great tip from Todd Whitaker (2001) in his book *Dealing with Difficult Parents: And Parents with Difficult Situations:* If you have not done anything wrong, but parents feel you have, you can sometimes soothe angry tempers by saying "I'm sorry this has happened." (Never add,"but you are wrong" or say that you were personally wrong when you weren't.) For instance, if a parent is upset about a student's grade and thinks it is your fault, say, "I am sorry about John's grade. We all need to work together to help John get the grade we know he can get when he works hard."
- ♦ Get to the point and stay focused.
- ♦ Empathize with parents' feelings.

◆ Ask meaningful questions that will steer the discussion in the direction of problem solving.

◆ Don't be defensive. "Unlearn" how to protect yourself, a concept that comes from the field of *action science.* A great suggestion from McEwan is to learn about action science from Chris Argyris (1986, 1991), noted organizational theorist.

◆ Speak quietly and make the right comments.

◆ Avoid being triangulated (caught between two people who should be dealing with each other instead of you). Sometimes divorced parents may triangulate their children or a teacher in their battle to discredit each other or to seek revenge.

◆ Give unpleasant information as gently as possible. Speak in simple terms and give specific examples. Let the examples speak for themselves. Do not judge or evaluate the student's behavior, just describe it.

◆ Welcome constructive criticism and respond to it graciously.

◆ Be understanding and supportive of parents who are also having trouble dealing with their child's behavior at home.

◆ Don't overreact or take parent's comments personally. Stay neutral and unemotional.

A great suggestion: If you feel yourself getting upset, make an excuse to leave the session for a few minutes. When you are by yourself, take several breaths, count to ten or to a hundred if you are really upset, and then return to the meeting feeling in better control.

◆ Consider cultural differences in communication styles and messages.

◆ If the meeting is dragging on and going nowhere, schedule another meeting and consider involving more people, including support staff who may be able to assist with the issues on which you might be stuck.

◆ Show parents clear evidence of student actions. For example if a student is reporting something inaccurately, reenact the situation so that parents can see what happened.

◆ Join with parents in defining and solving a school problem. Ask them for their support, for instance, in getting more resources for the school if they are complaining that their child is not getting what he needs.

- Suggest several options for dealing with issues. Allow parents to save face if necessary. Do not back them into a corner.
- Stay focused on the problems, not the personalities of the people involved.
- At the end of the conference, summarize what has been decided and conclude with a clear understanding of what each person intends to do to solve the problem.

McEwan says these are things not to do (p. 37–38):

- Don't interrupt.
- Don't try to change the subject without giving notice that you're about to do so.
- Never focus on things that cannot be changed.
- Don't start complaining about your own problems.
- Don't engage in silent combat (angry staring)
- Don't start rehearsing your answer before you have actually heard and understood what the parent is trying to communicate.
- Don't advise unless you've been asked.
- Don't try to persuade a parent that you are right and he or she is wrong.
- Don't try so hard to be neutral that you show no empathy.
- Don't come across as a know-it-all professional.
- Don't talk compulsively and over-explain.
- Don't let yourself get backed into a corner by an intimidating parent.
- Don't be so intent on smoothing a conflict that you achieve only a superficial resolution.

If you have a parent who is crazy, McEwan offers the following advice (pp. 38–40):

- Gather as much information as you can in order to understand the behaviors and motivation of the parent.
- Keep careful and complete notes about all your encounters with the parent.
- Keep superiors informed about what has gone on between you and the parent.
- Consult mental health professionals.
- Consult law enforcement professionals.

◆ Know your school board policies, the legal rights of parents and students, and your job description.

◆ Have a third party attend your meetings to take notes and witness the interaction between you and the parent.

◆ Be aware of the laws protecting the rights of children and your legal obligation to report any abuse of the children in your classes.

Another excellent resource to help you deal with the challenge of adversarial parents is to take the advice of William Ury in his book *Getting Past No: Negotiating Your Way from Confrontation to Cooperation* (1991/1993). Ury stresses the keys to effective negotiation: *getting ready* and *making join problem solving the goal*. Teachers must get ready for parent conferences. The more adversarial the conference or negotiation might be, the more prepared the teacher needs to be. Ury says that both sides of a negotiation can reach an agreement if they work together (side-by-side) to face the problem; however, there are five barriers to joint problem solving which I interpret in terms of parent-teacher relationships as follows:

1. *Your reactions:* The first and most important barrier lies within you. Human beings are reaction machines, and when we are under stress, we naturally feel like striking back.

2. *Parents' emotions:* I have already described how parents can feel angry, troubled, afraid, or crazy when they are perceiving a problem related to their child's well-being.

3. *Parents' position:* Parents may dig in and accept no alternatives. They may not know how to negotiate, and the only alternative they may understand is getting their way.

4. *Parents' dissatisfaction:* Parents may not see how any plan you might propose could solve the problem. They may not see how your proposals would benefit them or their child. And if it is your idea, they may refuse it for that reason alone.

5. *Parents' power:* If the parents see the negotiation as a win-lose proposition, they may feel determined to beat you by threatening your job or by getting their child out of your class. If the system allows them to get what they want without negotiating with you, why should they cooperate?

Ury says that even though stonewalling, attacks, and tricks are part of human nature when dealing with differences, you can negotiate your way through a problem by using five strategies to breakthrough those barriers in order to successfully negotiate resolution to a problem.

Here are the five breakthrough strategies in steps that correspond to the barriers just listed:

1. *Go to the Balcony:* The first barrier is your emotional reaction; therefore, you must get some emotional distance by getting off the stage and moving up to the balcony to get perspective on the issues. You should "go to the balcony" throughout the meeting if you feel your emotional reactions interfering with sound reasoning and communication.

2. *Step to Their Side:* The next barrier is their reactions; therefore, if you want to create the best climate for joint problem solving, do the opposite of what they expect (an emotional reaction). Listen carefully and respectfully to their side of the issue and acknowledge their perceptions.

3. *Reframe:* Again, do the opposite. If they dig in with their perception, do not argue or defend your position. Ask them to explain their side more so that you understand it better. Say, "Tell me more. Help me understand why you want that." Act as if you are partners in solving the problem, and that you are working on it from the same perspective.

4. *Build them a Golden Bridge:* If they are continuing to dig in with their perspective, do not push back. Show them a way to bridge the gap between their interests and yours. You need to help them save face and make the outcome look like a victory for them.

5. *Use Power to Educate:* If they are still uncooperative because they feel they can beat you at the power game, do not escalate (use threats and coercion); instead, show them that they cannot win by themselves and that they need your involvement.

(10) Suggestions for Dealing With Your Own School System

◆ You
  • Learn to understand clearly and sufficiently the family systems with which you are interacting.
  • Know the family systems that represent the students you teach so that you may deal with various pressures in an effective manner so that the child or children you share with their family will not be hurt.
  • Learn to respectfully interact with any family no matter how disagreeable they might be.

◆ Students
  • Be able to see that your students are members of a functional or dysfunctional family system, and that their behavior is affected not only by what happens in the classroom, but also by what happens in their homes or in their communities.
  • Be supportive of students by supporting their parents in their homes and communities and by truly inviting them into the school.
◆ Parents
  • If the parents of your students do not share your culture, learn about their culture.
  • Make sure your communication with parents is two-way.
  • Make sure you truly invite and utilize input from parents about what you are doing with their child.
◆ Administration
  • Encourage your school or school system leaders to invite parents to participate in leadership teams and other school decision-making activities.
  • Join with administration to interact with families to solve issues based on systemic thinking.
◆ Community
  • Encourage other stakeholders besides parents to help if you do not have a strong parent group.
  • Facilitate or work with other designated school personnel, such as counselors and social workers, to secure appropriate community services for your students' families who may be in need.

Summary

However you choose to deal with the challenge of underinvolved or adversarial parents, keep in mind that your failure to work out these issues may result in poor achievement for your students and stress for you. As with other challenges, you may choose to use a combination of ideas to develop your own plan, or you may choose to find out more information from the resources I have outlined. Remember these resources are mostly overviews, and if you want to learn the method and practice it, you should have a mentor or colleague who is familiar with the strategy to help you implement it. Keep in mind that working with families is a complex undertaking. It is important to fully understand what is behind a parent's underinvolvement or adversarial stance. Using systemic analysis can help you take into account all of the factors that have an impact on a problem with the family whose child you are teaching. Realizing that role understandings and cultural diversity can make parent-teacher relationships highly challenging can help you respond more effectively when problems arise. Using strategies to bring parents into schools and to improve the possibility that students will also learn at home will go a long way to prevent adversarial exchanges. However, if parents do approach you in an adversarial manner, you now have strategies to help you respond to them without feeling overwhelmed and defeated.

5

Tough Working Conditions

What Are the Challenges?

According to research, healthy and sound atmospheres for learning, or school cultures, "correlate strongly with increased student achievement and motivation, and with teacher productivity and satisfaction" (Stolp, 1994, p. 2). The conditions under which teachers and students work can present a major challenge usually because the working conditions in many schools are extremely disrespectful. Deborah Meier says in her book, *The Power of Their Ideas* (1996),

> I remember the first and most striking reaction I had to Chicago's South Side public schools—that they were (and probably still are) the most disrespectful environments, even for adults, that I had ever experienced.... I had no prior experience of being treated with such little respect or common courtesy, even as a child. (p. 124)

Many unfortunate teachers know exactly what Meier is talking about. A working environment can be disrespectful physically and/or emotionally and can create health problems for the victims of that disrespect.

I have divided this chapter into subtopics as follows: (1) Physical environment, (2) Time demands, (3) Organizational structures, (4) Evaluation of opposing views using the BESST Criterion, (5) Using the five pause-point system of decision making with a working conditions issue, and (6) Suggestions for solutions for your school system.

(1) Physical Environment

Challenges

Here are some typical conditions under which teachers work:

- ◆ Restroom: Teachers might be able to use the restroom between classes or during class if they can get someone to cover for them. The only time teachers are scheduled to use the restroom is during their planning period. Most schools in which I have worked have had no hot water available to wash hands.

◆ Temperature: Most schools have issues with temperature control. In some school systems, the heating and air conditioning are controlled by the district, and teachers have no heat and no air unless they have been turned on by someone "downtown." Many teachers have no ability to control the temperature in their rooms.

◆ Classrooms: Many classrooms are overcrowded with desks and/or tables, have poorly maintained wall coverings, and by the end of the day can look like a tornado came through them. Often custodians refuse to clean a teacher's room if she does not clean it first.

◆ Lunch: Most teachers have to eat with their students, or they have some kind of lunch duty. Many are allowed about 20 minutes to eat lunch while supervising students in an extremely noisy atmosphere.

◆ Telephone: Most teachers have extremely limited access to telephones in order to call parents or to make a personal call. Many schools have a limited number of telephone lines from which teachers may call out of their buildings.

◆ Supplies: Teachers often use their own money to supplement their limited teaching materials. In schools that serve a large number of children of poverty, students come to school ill prepared; therefore, teachers become responsible for supplying paper, pencils, and tissue for students who have colds.

◆ Safety: Although many teachers have little ability to lock up their belongings, school buildings have chains on doors and bars on windows to protect them from break-ins. These chains and bars suggest the atmosphere of a prison. Some schools in poor neighborhoods are surrounded by chain link fences topped with barbed wire. Schools are vulnerable to neighborhood violence and some teachers are afraid to work after sunset.

◆ Salary: It is well documented that teachers make less money than other equally educated and trained professionals. The tradition of paying teachers less money than equally educated and trained professionals may come from several sources. First, in the Middle Ages when schools were being established, it was illegal to pay teachers a salary for their work. Education was a gift from God and teachers were only paid by voluntary donations. Another source of substandard salary allotment includes the fact that for many years teachers were predominantly women, who were by law and by tradition second-class citizens. And finally, because teachers have summer off and seem to get off work in the early afternoon, the general population believes that teachers do not work a full day and do not deserve payment for a full day of work.

I could find very little information about the physical environment of schools or suggestions for what to do about these working conditions. It is obvious that the physical environment contributes to one's emotional well-being, and it has been proved that emotional well-being has an impact on learning. Clearly, to deal with many of these issues would take a major change in how policy makers allot money for education. Although some of these issues probably require a major shift in society's views of teachers and would probably require organized advocacy, there *are* some things teachers can do.

Solutions

Teachers can partner with community volunteers and parents. These partnerships can pressure policy makers to provide adequate funds to run a physically and emotionally safe school system. Teachers and community partners can also raise money and provide their time to improve the physical environment in schools. For instance, community volunteers and parents are great resources for school beautification and special grants that might address issues such as lack of telephones and technology. Some school advocates even find ways to provide needed supplies for students and teachers. Most members of a community are at least somewhat interested in children and their schools. Even though it may take some strategic fund raising, most communities and parents will say yes to reasonable requests for help. Strengthening the partnerships can significantly improve physical in schools.

(2) Time Demands

Challenges

One of the major issues associated with teachers' working conditions includes the demand on their *time* to do all that is expected of them. Teachers are expected to cover all of the content and skills associated with their school system's standard course of study. They are also expected to attend faculty meetings, professional development activities, and many other special meetings after school. Some teachers, in addition to teaching, are expected to coach, tutor, and mentor students after school. In addition to all of these activities, teachers are expected to call parents, meet with parents, grade papers, plan lessons, and deal with mounds of paperwork.

These time demands are extremely important in the first years of teaching when new teachers are learning their subject areas, how to deal with their students, and how to exist in a school. Time demands are also important for veteran teachers who are pressured to take leadership roles that can overwhelm them and burn them out.

Solutions

"Managing Time Demands" outlines some suggestions for dealing with these problems.

Managing Time Demands
Suggestions and Explanations of Suggestions

- Set a certain amount of time to do your work outside the classroom.

  This might include your planning period and some time after school. The amount of time after school is up to you; however, set that time according to *your* needs, not the *demands* of the job. I have heard of teachers staying up into the wee hours of the morning to accomplish a task. Is this reasonable? Who is asking them to do this? The bottom line is that if you are working constantly during the time you are in school and for that time you allot for after school (i.e., not wasting it socializing with peers or making personal calls), then you should be entitled to stop working at some point, even if the task is not complete. No one is expected to kill himself getting a job done. This is asking for burnout.

- Find a creative method to deal with administrative activities (such as copying, filing, posting information).

I have heard the suggestion that teachers should have assistants to help with their many activities that do not require direct teacher input. Until this happens (and it may never happen), teachers might use trustworthy parent or student helpers to assist with certain administrative activities, such as scoring multiple choice tests, putting grades in grade books or computer programs, running off materials, and other activities that do not require direct teacher input. I must emphasize that a parent or student helper must be completely trustworthy. If the helper is a student, it is preferable that she not be a member of your class. For instance, you might recruit a former student or a student highly recommended by another teacher. Helpers must be trusted not to discuss grades with other students. You may even need to inform parents that you have parent and/or student helpers and that you have had that helper or helpers sign a confidentiality statement of some sort. Parents can be concerned, and rightfully so, about another parent or student knowing their child's grades. Using a confidentiality form may help everyone feel secure that students are not being discussed inappropriately.

- Find a creative way to evaluate or grade student work.

In this age of accountability, teachers are expected to constantly assess students' knowledge and skills on objectives; however, this constant process of assessment can make the pile of papers grow at an unreasonable rate. For papers other than essays and other long answer tests (see the next section), I suggest the following:

1. Have students trade papers and grade short assessments (e.g., 5- to 10-question short-answer quizzes) in class. Short assessments help you know whether your students are learning the material. Grading these assessments in class frees the time you would take to grade them outside of class. Even more importantly, it helps with the review process.

2. Assign work that can be evaluated though oral presentation rather than in writing. You can avoid time evaluating students' work after school by evaluating oral reports and presentations as they are occurring in class. These kinds of assignments are helpful to students also because they are usually more authentic assessment methods, and they provide immediate feedback to you and to the students. Students should know on what points they are being evaluated (e.g., via a rubric that you provide) and you should have copies of the predetermined evaluation sheet or rubric on hand during their presentations. You should fill out the sheet as

students present and provide them with that completed feedback sheet (with a grade or level of achievement) shortly after they have made their presentation.

3. Find ways to use peer evaluations. For instance, if you believe students learn not only from you, but from each other, you can provide opportunities for students to offer feedback to each other about the quality of their work. Be careful with this strategy. You should take some time to help students learn to give appropriate feedback; for instance, asking students to grade each other can become a loyalty issue rather than truly helpful feedback. There are many helpful peer feedback strategies including PQP (Praise, Question, Perfect) or Three Kisses (praise statements) and a Wish (a statement to make the work better). Another caution about using peer evaluation is to make sure you do not overuse it. Students and parents want a significant amount of feedback from the teacher on the quality of the students' work.

4. Use multiple-choice tests that are easy to check. Some content areas make good use of multiple-choice tests, and they are certainly in line with the standardized tests on which students must be successful; however, many teachers believe multiple-choice questions cannot be used effectively as authentic assessment. Although multiple-choice questions should not be used exclusively to evaluate students' knowledge and skills, well-written multiple-choice questions can be highly challenging and useful as authentic assessment. The time you spend developing these kinds of assessments or evaluating the ones that might be provided for you by the makers of your teaching materials will save you time in the long run. They save time if you can reuse them and when you check them. (You can even use a scanner for further efficiency.)

5. Use group evaluations. Be careful with this one especially if students are highly competitive for grades. Never use group evaluations that might be unfair to the hard worker or let the slacker get by without doing his part.

■ Find a less time-consuming way to deal with students' writing.

One of the most labor intensive activities for a teacher is grading students' writing, whether it be for English, social studies, science, math (showing the work on a problem), or any subject area; however, assigning writing and giving students feedback about their writing is critical for student achievement. Here are two suggestions:

1. Ask students to keep a folder or portfolio of their work. There have been several books written about using portfolios for writing and you might do some research on different methods. To summarize: Ask students to keep a collection of their writing assignments or self-selected writing projects. You can also have students include answers to specific reflection questions you ask them about their writing at the beginning of the year and at the end. Ask students to choose a limited number of pieces of their writing on which you will provide feedback during the year and at the end. You may ask them to choose their pieces of writing based on specific criteria, for instance, asking them to include one expository piece, one narrative, and one poem. The other pieces in the portfolio may be self evaluated or peer evaluated.

2. Use self-evaluation or peer evaluation (for complete editing guides, see my book *Handbook on Differentiating Instruction in Middle and High Schools,* Northey, 2005). Ask students to evaluate their own papers or other students' papers through self-evaluation, partner evaluation, or small group evaluation. In self-evaluation, students reread their own papers; with partners, they trade papers; and with small groups, they pass papers to get a peer's paper to read. Next, give students editing sheets that require them to answer specific questions about their own work or other students' work. The questions can be both quantitative and qualitative. For instance, a quantitative question might be: How many primary source references are included in this report? A qualitative question might be: Based on the rubric, at what level does the writer prove the paper's thesis statement? Below standard, at standard, or above standard. Remember, however, that student writing must be assessed by you at some point. Do not choose to forgo writing assignments because evaluating them is time-consuming.

- If you are a new teacher, do all you can to avoid extra duties that require your time after school is over.

Although it may be highly appealing to be the coach of the cheerleaders or a member of the leadership team, you need to realize you will be experiencing a demanding year; you will need lots of time to process all you will be learning. Most administrators have been cautioned about loading new teachers with extra duty, but if your administrator has not heeded this advice, talk honestly with him about your need not to be overloaded. The bottom line for new teachers (in the first and even second year) is to fend off any external or internal pressure to jump into extra duties.

- If you are a veteran teacher leader and have become involved in too many committees and projects, make yourself say: "Thank you for the honor, but I think I'll have to say 'No thank you,' but I would suggest…" and let other teachers have the opportunities to take the honors.

  You can tell that demands for your time are getting into the danger zone if you are taking too much time away from your personal needs (family, friends, alone time) and the needs of your students. You know you have mismanaged your time if… (1) you begin feeling burned out and stressed-out by simple issues, (2) you feel you never enjoy time with your significant others, (3) you never get to read that novel sitting on your bedside table, (4) you let the papers pile up on your desk, or (5) you scale back on your work with your students because you're too busy helping to run the school or the district.

- Believe that your time as a professional teacher can be managed and that teaching does not have to take over your life.

  Whatever your situation, if you feel you are out of balance, talk to someone you can trust in order to work out a plan to make time work *for* you instead of *against* you. There are solutions. Teaching does not have to be so time-consuming.

(3) Organizational Structures

Challenges

According to a medieval curse "May you have to teach other people's children," teaching can be the ultimate condemnation (Barth, 1990). The teaching profession has developed the reputation for being too difficult and underpaid, and it is experiencing a crisis in retention and recruitment. This fact has forced communities and lawmakers to search for answers as to why schools are losing teachers and having trouble replacing them. According to Barth (1990), too many schools are extremely difficult places to work, and as a matter of fact, the organizational structure of some schools works against the important processes, collaboration and open communication, that form the best environment for student achievement (p. 27). Barth reports that in a study he conducted teachers at a respected suburban high school expressed the following feelings (p. 12):

- ◆ Discontent and malaise: Teachers felt unsupported, undervalued, unappreciated, overworked, underpaid, and not respected by the community.

- ◆ Pervasive lack of trust: Not trusting colleagues, principals, parents, and not feeling trusted by the community.
- ◆ Isolation and compartmentalization: Having to compete for resources and for the best students.
- ◆ Helpless and powerless: Feeling no ability to make a difference or to change their situation.
- ◆ Frustration with too much to do: Especially noninstructional duties.

Barth is convinced that the most important relationship in the schoolhouse is the relationship between the principal and the teachers, and if that relationship is adversarial, the school is not a healthy place for adults, young people or children. Many schools are not healthy. They do not provide the structure that allows all participants to deal with the challenge of educating a diverse group of children and young people. Here are some factors that describe an unhealthy school culture (adapted from McEwan, 1998):

- A lack of respect pervades the building. Everyone complains about everyone else and most feel they have no ability to handle situations effectively. Adults yell at each other and at students. People are sarcastic, critical and negative.
- A sense of powerlessness to make a difference about most issues.
- Strict and impermeable boundaries between students and teachers and teachers and principals.
- Principals consider differences of opinion as a threat to their authority.
- The principal is under-involved and uninterested in many problems experienced by teachers, students and parents.
- The principal lacks useful skills for establishing positive relationships with diverse groups of teachers, students and parents.
- Morale is low and the principal does not seem to be aware of that fact or care to address it if he/she is aware of it.
- The lack of unity among the staff leads to competition, cliques, destructive criticism, and quarreling.
- Recognizing achievement is not a priority and rarely occurs.

- Honest and open communication does not occur. It could be dangerous to say what you truly believe; therefore, people only talk behind closed doors to their friends about their deeply held concerns.
- One person runs the school.
- People deny the existence of conflict.
- People work on their own agendas and goals; there is little teaming and sharing of ideas and resources.
- People do not ask for help because they might be seen as incompetent. There is no interdependence.
- Individual differences are not respected.

What are the causes of these unpleasant organizational tendencies? Sergiovanni (1996) and Senge (2000) suggest that most schools are still organized by unproductive and outdated theories as follows: The Pyramid Theory and the Railroad Theory. See the following chart for descriptions:

Pyramid Theory	Railroad Theory
One person at the top controls the work of those at the bottom. All workers at the bottom embrace and produce the vision developed by that person. The product that is produced is standardized.	The leadership develops the best way to get several jobs done in a standard way. The tracks are laid that will deal with all problems and accomplish the goals of the organization. Workers merely need to be taught the system in order to get the job done.

Solutions

Instead of being mired in these outdated industrial model theories, many school leaders look to more enlightened business models such as Total Quality Management, the Baldridge System, and the Balanced Score Card. These models demonstrate great ideas for how people might work together efficiently and collaboratively to satisfy customers, create new products, and build ever increasing productivity and profits. Some of these models have been clearly adapted and revised for use in school systems with great effect. Business leaders and policy makers can often see the benefits of these systems more keenly than other models because they believe schools should be run like good businesses. But does that work? Are schools organizations that can be run like businesses?

Sergiovanni (1996) in his book *Leadership for the Schoolhouse*, strongly encourages educators to avoid using some business models to organize or solve problems in schools. He says we might borrow some good ideas from the business community, but schools are just *not* like businesses. Sergiovanni says that schools should be thought of as extended families where teachers and administrators stand *in loco parentis* for their students. Therefore, the goals of the school are focused on lovingly meeting the needs of every child who comes to learn. He makes an excellent case for smaller schools that allow every child to be well known by at least one caring adult. His suggestion for large schools is that they plan smaller sub-schools within them; for instance the 9th grade could have its own building where every 9th grader feels connected with other 9th graders and the teachers who teach them.

Deborah Meier (1995, 2002) also makes a strong case for smaller schools. She founded schools in east Harlem that have proved the value of smaller schools and the benefits of promoting democratic values in school. Meier explains in her book, *The Power of Their Ideas* that small schools without top-down administrators can work, but that it is not easy and it takes much more time than a weekly faculty meeting. She explained that there were times when it might have seemed easier to have a top-down supervisor to solve a problem, someone to blame if it didn't work, but that in the long run, sticking to democratic values that required complete collaborative decision making paid off in terms of student achievement and teacher satisfaction.

Sergiovanni (1996), Senge (1990 & 2000), Meier (1995, 2002) and many others have encouraged education stakeholders o change outdated and unenlightened views of what works in schools. Senge (even though Senge also comes from the business community, his model is more a philosophy of learning than of building a business) in his books *The Fifth Discipline* (1990) and *Schools that Learn* (2000) offers an alternative to authoritarian hierarchies with his conceptualization of the "5 disciplines": (1) personal mastery, (2) mental models, (3) building shared vision,(4) team learning, and (5) systems thinking.

These disciplines work together to structure learning organizations or communities in which much can be accomplished. They are not developed in any particular order, but I will start with (1) *personal mastery*. Senge (2000) describes personal mastery as a "set of practices" that work together in a "both and" fashion to support an idealistic vision while also considering the reality with which you are faced. This part of the discipline concerns looking inward to see who you are and what you want in your life while being acutely aware of the world with which you must deal in order to realize your dreams. Personal mastery requires that you make choices based on your values. Some of these choices may take courage and may require you to constantly challenge your thinking as you deepen and expand your vision for yourself and your organization. (pp. 59–65).

Next is (2) *mental models*, which Senge describes as being just below our awareness and can limit a person's ability to change. These mental models sometimes cause us to "climb the ladder of inference" or jump to conclusions about someone's behavior or something someone says. When we misperceive a situation, we begin to let our misperception influence what data we select to believe for all future interactions. If this happens, you get into what Senge calls a "reflexive loop" that if not challenged, can cause you to draw faulty conclusions that might interfere with your ability to collaborate effectively with your colleagues (pp. 66–71).

The next idea is (3) *shared vision*, which Senge says cannot be sustained if based on the dictate of an authority. When people are creating a shared vision, they must feel free to express their honest opinions about that vision, and they must not fear any repercussions from what they might say to a superior. Administrator and supervisor must not attempt to put limits on this process or they will not get ownership of the vision.

This is not an easy process; it takes strategy, time and carefulness (pp. 71–73).

Idea (4) is *team learning*, which over time gets people who work in a team to thinking and act together. This does not mean that they all think alike, but it does mean that they think and act as a unit. Dialogue is the cornerstone of effective team learning. In dialogue, members suspend their assumptions about various issues and look at them from different perspectives. A typical dialogue might have the following steps: 1. Surfacing assumptions – thinking about your beliefs before you talk about them. 2. Displaying assumptions – speaking about your ideas so that others may know what you are thinking. 3. Inquiry – inviting others to explore issues with you; to challenge old views and learn new ways of thinking and behaving. Senge suggests that you meet at least 3 times to decide if you can work well together, and you might consider having a facilitator (pp. 73–77).

Finally, (5) *systems thinking*, which simply stated is "developing awareness of complexity, interdependencies, change and leverage" (p. 77). Systemic thinking, according to Senge "provides a different way of looking at problems and goals- not as isolated events but as components of larger structures."(p. 78) Systemic thinking involves observing events, noticing patterns or trends, determining the structure of the system, examining your mental models, and determining leverage points. Systems are nonlinear and can be conceptualized as causal loops; they seek balance and can resist change. The most effective conceptualization of systemic intervention is the double loop model for doing the following for problem solving: observing, reflecting, reconnecting, reframing, deciding, reconsidering, doing. (See figure below from Senge, p. 96)

Systemic Intervention's Double Loop Model

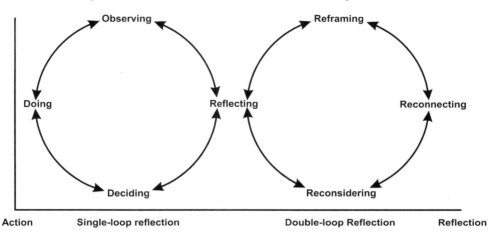

Action   Single-loop reflection   Double-loop Reflection   Reflection

Solutions

Eaker, Dufour, and Dufour (2002) promote the idea of shifting the way schools are organized from traditional models to professional learning communities. In their book, *Getting Started: Restructuring Schools to Become Professional Learning Communities,* they provide excellent comparisons that represent cultural shifts between traditional schools and a professional learning community. They state that if these shifts do not occur, a professional learning community cannot be formed at your school. The basic comparison is as follows:

Learning Communities	Traditional Hierarchy Models
Decision making and goal setting are shared processes; community focus is on learning.	Decisions are made by supervisors who require those under them to comply with directives.

What follows is a list of specific comparison statements regarding what must be addressed if a cultural shift is to occur. The categories, from Eaker, Dufour, and Dufour (pp. 10–28), are as follows:

Comparison Statements Showing Cultural Shifts

FROM ——————————————————————————————➤ TO

Collaboration

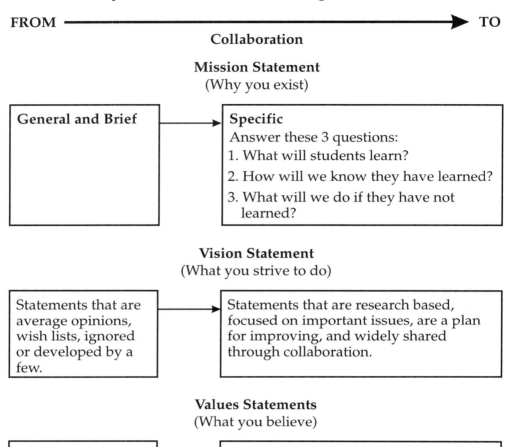

Mission Statement
(Why you exist)

General and Brief	**Specific** Answer these 3 questions: 1. What will students learn? 2. How will we know they have learned? 3. What will we do if they have not learned?

Vision Statement
(What you strive to do)

Statements that are average opinions, wish lists, ignored or developed by a few.	Statements that are research based, focused on important issues, are a plan for improving, and widely shared through collaboration.

Values Statements
(What you believe)

Values that are random, self-serving, excessive, and stated as beliefs.	Values that are connected to the vision, spoken in terms of behaviors and commitment, few in number, and constitute a plan for school improvement.

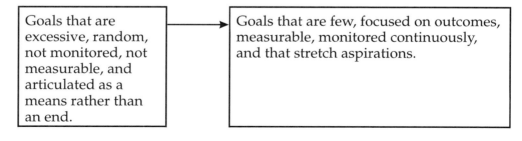

Goal Statements
(What you want to accomplish)

Goals that are excessive, random, not monitored, not measurable, and articulated as a means rather than an end.	Goals that are few, focused on outcomes, measurable, monitored continuously, and that stretch aspirations.

Focus on Learning

| Teaching | → | Learning |

Curriculum

| Teachers making individual decisions about what to teach and who teaches it. | → | Collaborative plans that address curriculum, reduce coverage, and improve depth; collaborative assessment processes; and a solid plan for addressing students who are not learning. |

Collective Inquiry

| Decisions made by averaging opinion. | → | Decisions made by research-based decision making and exploring best teaching practices. |

Research and Results

| External approval of strategies and doing what teachers like best. | → | Evaluating effectiveness internally though action research and examining the effect of teaching practices have on student achievement. |

Leadership

| Administrators as leaders and teachers as followers. | → | Everyone as a leader in some way. |

School Improvement Plan

| A large number of items and the emphasis on getting it done. | → | Focus on a few critical items that become the mechanism for school reform. |

Celebration

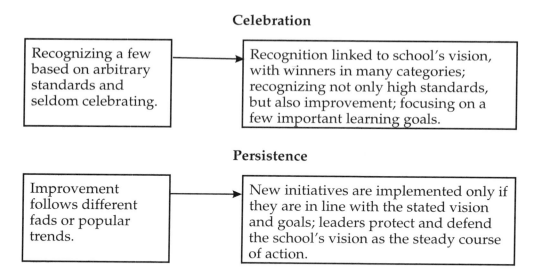

Recognizing a few based on arbitrary standards and seldom celebrating.	Recognition linked to school's vision, with winners in many categories; recognizing not only high standards, but also improvement; focusing on a few important learning goals.

Persistence

Improvement follows different fads or popular trends.	New initiatives are implemented only if they are in line with the stated vision and goals; leaders protect and defend the school's vision as the steady course of action.

Although Senge and Eaker and Dufour have somewhat different descriptions of learning communities, here is my synthesis of the types of features a learning community should have:

- ◆ A united vision organizes the behavior of the group.
- ◆ Everyone is a learner and everyone is a leader.
- ◆ All views and opinions are respectfully addressed.
- ◆ Communication is open, honest, and respectful.
- ◆ Everyone is equal, but different people have different roles, all of which are equally important to the community's well being.
- ◆ Problems are solved collaboratively.
- ◆ Achievement is celebrated often.
- ◆ Everyone supports the vision for the community.
- ◆ Differences of opinion are aired and discussed openly and respectfully.
- ◆ Ethics, morality and virtue are measures for decision-making.
- ◆ Decision-making is collaborative.
- ◆ Everyone focuses on positive results that should flow as a result of inquiry (i.e. research on best practices) and collaboration.
- ◆ Humanism and democracy form the basis of the community.
- ◆ All members trust that the community is intellectually safe.
- ◆ Members have conversations or dialogue about issues rather than discussions.

- Members practice keeping open minds and avoid jumping to conclusions or stereotyping.
- The goal of leaders is to help others get their needs met and to help others also become leaders.
- Members think systemically (i.e. see patterns and interrelationships among parts of the system).
- Members believe in the power of the collective intelligence of team work.

(4) Evaluation of Opposing Views Based on the BESST Criterion = Value Added

We can use the BESST Criterion to evaluate the traditional hierarchy and the learning communities models.

BESST Criterion = Value Added

Brain-Based	Ethical	Standards	Systems Theory
In an environment where students' goals are aligned with classroom experiences, the brain motivates itself to learn without being bribed by rewards or threatened by punishment.	All people (including children) are created equal with equal rights to freedom, happiness, and the Golden Rule.	Extensive skills and knowledge help teachers provide a positive learning environment.	Having an awareness of the interactions that make up an environment helps teachers respectfully and strategically plan their actions.

- *Brain-Based:* Brain-based research supports learning communities over the traditional hierarchy model because it supports the notion of a positive environment in which achievement can occur. If you assume teachers achieve more when working conditions are less stressful and punitive, you would say that learning communities strive to eliminate threat more than traditional hierarchies. In traditional hierarchies, there is always the possibility that an administrator will abuse his power over employees so that the free flowing ability to meet challenges is less likely to occur.

◆ *Ethics:* Traditional hierarchies are firmly rooted in the conventional level of ethical development where rules are made by authority figures and compliance is required under threat of punishment or reprisal. Learning communities are much more likely to allow for Golden Rule behavior because they are concerned with building consensus in order to meet the needs of all involved.

◆ *Standards:* The standards movement is more supportive of learning communities because it assumes that all stakeholders of an education system should have the skills and knowledge to make important and responsible decisions about student learning. Believing that all students can learn and valuing collaboration among all stakeholders are definitely learning community characteristics.

◆ *Systems Theory:* Learning communities promote shared decision making, which allows teachers and other stakeholders to develop ownership of their school's goals, vision, and activities. The traditional model allows supervisors to dictate what is nonnegotiable to their "inferiors." This model does not respect all stakeholders and does not promote ownership.

◆ = *Value Added:* The learning community model adds value to the lives of all involved because each member has an equal and respected share in the benefits and challenge of the work of the school.

(5) Using the Five Pause-Points System of Decision Making with a Working Conditions Issue

(1. Planning, 2. Implementing/Observing, 3. Reflection, 4. Revision, and 5. Acting with More Knowledge)

P1—Planning an Action: As Academic Facilitator, I was required to provide a professional development session for the teachers with whom I worked. My task was to "train" the teachers to use several strategies that the district had decided would be "best practices." The ideas were useful and interesting; however, these teachers were in various phases of their profession and were not be too interested in being "trained." One of them had decided to stop teaching middle school; another was planning to leave teaching altogether (she did not even attend the session). The others were enthusiastic, but had their own ways of doing things. I decided to very briefly explain the strategies the district required, and then to facilitate a discussion based on the teachers' agenda.

1. Was my action in line with brain-based research? For instance did I need to use bribery or punishment and were my goals aligned with teachers', principals', and the district's goals?

   Even though the district was promoting certain strategies, its major goal, which was also the goal of our administrative team, was related to student achievement. I felt that aligning the goals of my required session with the teachers' own goals would promote their commitment to working together to address student achievement goals. I did not want to "require" them to follow a directive and I certainly did not feel it would be productive to find a way to bribe them to follow the directive or punish them if they did not.

2. Would I hurt anyone or help anyone if I allowed teachers to determine their own agenda?

   As stated earlier, I trusted these teachers to demonstrate high levels of professionalism, and I did not want to in any way assume that I knew better than they what we should discuss. I felt that our working together collaboratively would benefit everyone, especially the students they taught.

3. Was this action in line with the standards? Did it show skill and knowledge and create a positive atmosphere?

   In this type of session I could demonstrate skill as a facilitator, which required me to encourage others to share ideas rather than dominating the conversation. Even though I had as many or more ideas than my fellow teachers, I felt it was more important for them to show what they knew.

4. Was my action sensitive to the system it affected?

   My school system is top-down with few opportunities for true collegiality; however, because I was "in charge," I was able to do as I pleased. I needed to be careful to attend to the systems' "required" paper work so that I could continue to have opportunities to conduct professional development in this manner. If I blatantly disregarded the system's "nonnegotiables" I would find it difficult to continue in a leadership role at all.

5. What did I do?

   I held the session on a teacher workday.

P2—Implementation/Observation: After briefly presenting the system's nonnegotiables, I asked the teachers what burning issues they wanted to deal with collaboratively. They were eager to share ideas, analyze test data, and make specific plans to address students' learning deficiencies. I showed them that I could learn a great deal from them. Allowing other teachers to demonstrate their strength showed that as a leader, I was not competitive or jealous of their abilities, and that I was comfortable with sharing leadership. We worked several hours and accomplished a great deal.

P3—Reflection:

1. Did I need to use bribery or punishment?

    I did not need bribery or punishment to get these professional teachers to do what they knew they needed to do to improve their own practice for the benefit of their students. I trusted in their integrity, knowledge, and skills.

2. Did I help anyone or hurt anyone?

    I think this collaborative session helped these teachers address the needs *they* identified for our students, not the needs identified by our district that had little understanding of the specific needs of our student population.

3. Did I demonstrate knowledge and skill?

    I demonstrated knowledge of methods for developing collaborative problem-solving sessions and skills of facilitating those kinds of sessions. It takes restraint to keep one's ego under control in order to let others share leadership and authority.

4. Did I consider the system I was affecting?

    Although the system may not have totally sanctioned what I did, I did not blatantly disregard its requirements. The results of our working together met the needs of the system in spirit if not in absolute compliance.

P4—Revision: No revisions were needed and I planned to conduct all sessions in this manner.

P5—Acting with More Knowledge—Value Added: It was truly wonderful to experience the joy of collaborating with committed and professional colleagues. We all improved our knowledge and skills as we focused on how to help our students learn. Having a session like this one made me even more discouraged with traditional professional development programs that violate what research has proved works best for adult learners.

(6) Suggestions for Dealing With Your Own School System

Think about...

◆ Yourself

Make sure you understand how systems work. If you think you need to know more, make a plan to learn about systems theory. As I said in Chapter 1, teachers use systems theory all the time when they do things like make a seating chart based on how their students interact, but most could learn more.

Find a mentor who knows about systemic thinking and get help to practice thinking and acting based on the system.

Examine your roles at your school to determine if the working conditions need to be improved. Think about your sphere of influence and join with others who have similar views to discus what you can do.

If you are a victim of oppression or abuse, take action against the abusive system but do not become an oppressor or abuser yourself.

Develop self-awareness about how issues such as time demands and other work demands are affecting your ability to do your job well; if you are not performing as you feel you should, work with someone you trust to help you adjust what you are doing before, during, and after school.

◆ Students

Understand how your students are affected by your poor working conditions or unhealthy school culture. Plan ways to work toward making your classroom an oasis from the negativity.

Make sure you work with students to facilitate student leadership and democracy in your classroom.

Look at the physical environment of your classroom and realize the interaction of that environment with your students' achievement and attitudes.

◆ Parents

See the value of joining with parents in the struggle for improved working conditions. The potential power of this alliance could shake up the system in a major way. (Parents and teachers, however, have yet, in many cases, to find a powerful way to get on the same side of this issue.)

Get involved in a leadership team that includes parents, teachers, and administrators.

◆ Administration

If your school or district is based on a heavy-handed top-down bureaucracy, you are at a great disadvantage; however, all is not hopeless. One good thing about being a teacher is that the door to your classroom can be closed. But you must take some action; if you do not ask for a collaborative system, you will never get one.

◆ Community

Discover ways can you help the community understand the effect of poor working conditions on the health of your school.

Enlist community volunteers to help improve physical working conditions.

Ask community volunteers to advocate for better salaries and better school resources.

Ask community volunteers to help with special school projects that will improve working conditions.

Summary

Working conditions for teachers and school environments for students can improve; however, far too many school systems continue to allow disrespectful practices and to organize around models that are not working. We know that when a school loses a significant number of teachers each school year, something must be wrong. The solutions are complex and may require major shifts in ideology and practice coming simultaneously from many directions. Better funding will also help. All of the best ideas for reorganizing schools so that the conditions are better for teachers, administrators, parents, and their students must be funded. These ideas can bubble up from the community of teachers, students, and parents or they can come from directives made by policy makers, superintendents, and principals. Rarely, if ever, does a school system exist in other than a top-down hierarchy. For instance, Deborah Meier, discussed at the beginning of this chapter, could not have developed her special teacher-led program without permission from above, her superintendent. Top-down hierarchies that dominate our school systems continue to ignore poor working conditions, but they must be addressed if we want to provide excellent learning environments for all students and ultimately for the future of our nation.

6

Solutions Overview

Even though I have offered solutions along the way, you may still not be sure how you want to deal with these four challenges and others. As a form of overview and in order to help you decide what to do, in this chapter I provide (1) An overview of the opposing views of the four challenges, (2) An evaluation of opposing views using the BESST Criterion, (3) A model for a caring-based organization versus a traditional school model, and (4) A presentation of other ideas that may be of interest to you as you deal with challenges in your school.

(1) Overview of the Opposing Views of the Four Challenges

In the four areas of challenge—discipline, unmotivated students, underinvolved or adversarial parents, and tough working conditions—there are theories and practices that line up at opposing ends of a spectrum of choices of educational models that range from traditional hierarchies to organizations characterized by mutuality and collaboration. See "Spectrum of Educational Models" to get an overview of these differences.

Spectrum of Educational Models

Traditional Hierarchy Models ——▶ Mutuality/Collaboration Models	
Discipline	
Authoritarian models that put ——▶ the teacher solidly in control of the students' behavior.	Learning community models that include student meetings and student-shared responsibility for the well-being of the classroom.
Unmotivated Students	
Objectivism: Information must ——▶ flow through the teacher to the students. The teacher is the only expert.	Constructivism: Students struggle with information to create meaning. The teacher is a facilitator.

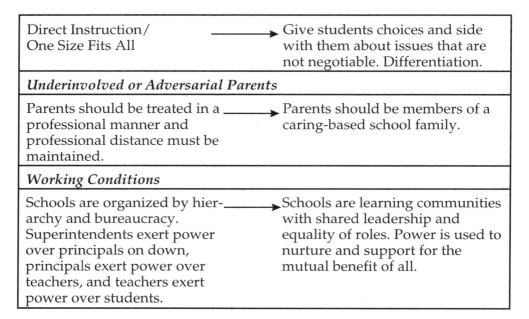

Direct Instruction/ One Size Fits All	⟶	Give students choices and side with them about issues that are not negotiable. Differentiation.
Underinvolved or Adversarial Parents		
Parents should be treated in a professional manner and professional distance must be maintained.	⟶	Parents should be members of a caring-based school family.
Working Conditions		
Schools are organized by hierarchy and bureaucracy. Superintendents exert power over principals on down, principals exert power over teachers, and teachers exert power over students.	⟶	Schools are learning communities with shared leadership and equality of roles. Power is used to nurture and support for the mutual benefit of all.

Have you decided which side of the spectrum you prefer? Or, are you somewhere in the middle? If you see yourself in the middle, how did you find a middle ground? It may help you to review some ideas about how to apply the BESST Criterion as you make decisions about how to deal with the four challenges. In this chapter, I model for you how I analyze the issues involved when making decisions about how to face these challenges in my own school. I encourage you to follow a similar procedure from your perspective.

(2) Evaluation of Opposing Views Based on the BESST Criterion = Value Added

Step 1: Review the Elements of the BESST Criterion.

BESST Criterion = Value Added

Brain-Based	Ethical	Standards	Systems Theory
In an environment where students' goals are aligned with classroom experiences, the brain motivates itself to learn without being bribed by rewards or threatened by punishment.	All people (including children) are created equal with equal rights to freedom, happiness, and the Golden Rule.	Extensive skills and knowledge help teachers provide a positive learning environment.	Having an awareness of the interactions that make up an environment helps teachers respectfully and strategically plan their actions.

Step 2: Analysis

Analyze how BESST Criterion might be used to think about solutions to the four challenges. The following pages show how I would proceed.

The Discipline Challenge

B Discipline strategies that reflect brain-based research are aligned with students' goals, and therefore avoid reward and punishment.

E Strategies that demean students in any way or take away rights that are promised within our democratic values should be avoided.

S Teachers should learn a variety of discipline strategies that suit their own needs and that are fair to all students.

ST Discipline strategies should be devised in the context of the needs of the classroom and the school. Teachers should learn to promote change through a careful analysis of the relationships among students and all adults within and throughout the school, family, and community.

= Value Added Choosing appropriate discipline strategies and implementing them well will assure a valuable learning environment for students and teachers.

The Unmotivated Student Challenge

B   Students are not motivated appropriately by external rewards and punishment; therefore any effective strategy should rely on inspiring students to motivate themselves by carefully aligning teaching activities with students' goals.

E   Respectful and effective motivational strategies offer choices and ask students to understand and cooperate with activities that they might not perceive as valuable or fun but which may be necessary from the perspective of community values.

S   Teachers should use best practices that encourage students to develop ownership of classroom activities and goals. They should avoid strategies that allow students to be passive participants in the process.

ST Teachers should analyze their classroom activities to note which activities promote student participation (motivation). They should never let a student drop out of the education process without doing all they can to find ways to reach any child who may appear unmotivated.

= Value Added   If strategies promote motivation in all students, there should be no discipline or achievement issues.

The Underinvolved or Adversarial Parent Challenge

B   Parents should be genuinely welcomed into the school. They must feel that you are respectful of their sincere feelings about their child's participation in your classroom and must not feel bribed to participate in school activities. They must not sense fear or arrogance from you based on class differences.

E   Your stance toward families requires that you treat all parents with equal respect.

S   Your choice of behaviors toward the parents of your students must demonstrate a willingness to learn all you can about their perspectives so that you might best serve them and their child.

ST You must be clear about your role in how you relate to the families of your students. If you do not or are not able to see your students' families as part of the school family, you will need to find other ways to show caring and concern for their children as well as content knowledge. You must understand how students are affected by their families.

= Value Added   Parents' positive participation in their child's school is the best predictor of student achievement. Whether you keep professional distance or see the parents of your students as part of the school family, you need to keep them involved as a major part of your job.

Working Conditions Challenges

B   Positive working conditions would not include bribery or punishment of the faculty. They are both disrespectful processes and should not be a part of any school program. Adults and students at all levels should regularly acknowledge achievement in many forms and contexts.

E   No one in a school should be treated disrespectfully or unfairly by anyone else.

S   To improve working conditions, accomplished teachers should take leadership roles that promote partnerships with the administration, community volunteers, students, and parents.

ST Teachers should understand how their school system is organized so that they might have an important voice in making the school a great place to be.

= Value Added   Working conditions will improve when respect and democratic values are firmly upheld by everyone in the school and outside the school.

(3) Caring-Based Versus Traditional Education Organizations

A caring based educational organization might be vastly different from the traditional education model. (See "Traditional Education Model.") The latter model starts with superintendents at the top and ends with students at the bottom. Parents and community stakeholders apply pressure from the *outside.* An emphasis on test scores competition, grades, and reward and punishment form the basis for the school to exist.

Traditional Education Model

A caring-based education organization includes two groups of stakeholders whose roles differ, but who work side by side. (See "Caring-Based Education Model.") First, the roles of teacher, parent, student, and administrator, though vastly different, are equal in value for the mutual benefit of everyone in the organization. No one because of his or her role could have negative power over another person. Power is used to nurture and support, not to judge and control. Decision making is shared among all who are affected by those decisions. In contrast to the one-way flow of power in the traditional model, in the caring-based model, power flows back and forth among all participants. (See the arrows in both diagrams.)

Caring-Based Education Model

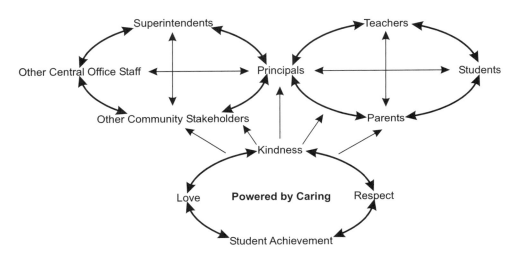

Second, the superintendent, deputy superintendents, curriculum and instruction and other middle managers, and other stakeholders including policy makers and business leaders work somewhat separately but in collaboration with the school-based personnel. These people relate directly to the principal as the administrator whose role might be to act as a liaison between the central office and the school personnel. Of course, all school-level personnel have access to this other group, but, for the sake of efficiency, the principal may be the best choice for conveying messages back and forth. Messages are in the form of ideas and suggestions rather than nonnegotiable dictates and directives. Arrows point both ways among all participants in this group with connection through the principal.

As I mention previously, some kinds of effective checks and balances should be implemented to work against the natural tendency of certain types of people—in the animal kingdom, they are called alpha males or alpha females—to exert power over any one else. Checks and balances might include a teacher/student/parent/administration counsel that is promoted and supported by the central office group and stakeholders.

Presently, many schools have leadership teams. This is an excellent idea, but most leadership teams have little impact on abuses of power in the school. Members of a leadership team might make it clear that they will use the positive power of nurture and support to protect victims of abuse from that abuse. Of course, their protection would be provided in a caring manner, which would include counseling with and educating an offender to do a better job of containing her needs to control and abuse power. The superintendent group could promote and support checks and balances to keep other groups honest in their commitment to collaboration.

Members of the caring-based educational organization might have the following descriptions (realizing that the role descriptions would inevitably be decided by the learning community):

- Administrators would conscientiously develop expertise in all administrative issues related to the running of the school.

- Parents would develop expertise in what works best with their child/children and would learn ways to support the school and specific teachers' classrooms.

- Students would develop the ability to control their behavior for the benefit of the group and would set serious learning goals for themselves.

- Teachers would constantly and continuously develop expertise in teaching skills and their content areas for the benefit of the learning community.

- Central office personnel would refrain from sending ideas as directives and would make certain their ideas gain ownership by those who will implement them.

These positions in the organization would be powered by caring. This caring would be revealed in elements such as kindness, respect, student achievement, and love.

From all I have learned as I read about how to deal with the four challenges, it seems to me that the best solutions to these challenges would be enhanced in an organization that is caring-based.

(4) Other Challenges and Solutions

What follows are some additional challenges and solutions.

New Teachers

Many schools/districts are organized to support and nurture new teachers; however, many are not. In her article "Common Space, Common Time, Common Work," Melody J. Shank (2005) states that many new teachers are subjected to hazing, which she defines as follows: to harass by requiring unnecessary or disagreeable work, by using ridicule or criticism, or as an initiation into a group. She lists a "Recipe for Disaster" (Shank, p. 23) as follows:

◆ Teaching more than two preps.

◆ Teaching mainly ninth-grade courses in schools where these are the most challenging courses to teach.

◆ Teaching mainly entry-level courses (such as Spanish I, Introduction to Biology, and Algebra I).

◆ Teaching in more than one classroom.

◆ Teaching new courses with little or no developed curriculum.

◆ Getting hired late (end of summer or after the school year starts).

◆ Holding substandard credentials and/or not having majored in the subject that they are teaching.

◆ Being provided with an inadequate supply of books for their students.

◆ Having a classroom located away from the classrooms of other members of their department.

◆ Being evaluated late in the year.

◆ Being asked to run time-consuming clubs.

◆ Not being represented on decision-making committees.

Many first-year teachers have reported that they were victims of this "hazing recipe." Too often beginning teachers are assigned to the most challenging schools; no wonder they leave this kind of thoughtless system.

Testing

Assessment, accountability, and monitoring are not bad in themselves, but some of us seem to have lost perspective about their benefits and have probably inadvertently used them in some cases for harm rather than for good. As a teacher, you can protect yourself and your students from the ills of testing by making sure you have not overreacted to its pressures. If your attitude about testing is appropriate, you will most likely be able to help your students develop an appropriate attitude toward testing too. See the following chart for appropriate and inappropriate responses to testing:

Appropriate Response to Testing	Inappropriate Response to Testing
Tests help teachers understand specific skills and content the community wants students to learn in each grade level.	Tests reflect only the skills and content a teacher should teach her students.
Teachers and students should do their best in terms of preparing for and taking tests.	Teachers and students should put extreme pressure on themselves for fear of failing the tests.
Tests help parents and community members evaluate certain aspects of a school or district.	Poor test results mean that the school, its teachers, principals, and students do not work hard enough and do not know enough to be successful.
Students should understand that tests help them know their level of achievement in specific areas.	Students believe that their performance on a specific test indicates whether they are smart or stupid.
Poor performance is kept in perspective so that students' self-esteem is not negatively affected.	Excellent performance is rewarded and poor performance is subtly or obviously punished.

Closing the Gap

Another issue that has been hotly debated among educators is the issue of closing the gap between middle-class and poor students. Robert Evans makes one of the best arguments in his article, "Reframing the Achievement Gap" (2005). He says that educators basically congregate in two camps: One group believes there is little if anything schools can do to compensate for the effects of socioeconomic status on the achievement of students, and the other group, which seems to have won the argument, says that all children can learn and that schools can make a tremendous difference in the lives of *all* students. The truth probably lies somewhere between these two camps. Policy makers, school leaders, and the community put tremendous pressure on teachers to assure that low-performing students pass the test. They prey on the pride some educators feel about their potential for shaping the lives of their students. These unrealistic expectations from can drive teachers from the classroom. According to Evans, a teacher at most has access to 10% of a student's life, so it can be difficult to make a difference. Teachers cannot completely compensate for overwhelming negative influences in some students' lives, especially if the child himself has given up. Instead of trying to accomplish the impossible, teachers and other educators might set realistic goals that could include increasing the number of involved community resources and teaming with other stakeholders, such as churches, counselors, social services, and mental health services.

In one district, school programs have developed partnerships with social workers and mental health workers who have helped students learn how to deal with behavior issues. In some cases, more than half of the students had fewer office referrals if they were working with a therapist. Also, a school was paired with a similar school to determine if these partnerships worked. The school that received the services from the community had a significant decrease in suspensions, whereas the other school had no major changes. Schools alone cannot raise a child; it may truly "take a village."

Many successful teachers consider the issue of closing the gap as a problem with the system, and thereby avoid the trap that makes them believe that they have to be miracle workers. They know they cannot reverse some situations by themselves; therefore, they join with others to collaborate about students' lack of achievement. In other words, these successful teachers never give up on a child; instead, they *allow* themselves to get help.

The Grating Paradox

According to the Constitution, we all have the right to freedom of speech, but this right is not enforced in schools. In some schools, a teacher with outspoken opinions might find herself at odds with a principal, and then find she is scheduled to teach the worst classes and has been assigned the worst duties. Or a feisty student who disagrees with a teacher might find himself getting an F on a paper that reflects ideas unacceptable to that teacher. In order to reverse this suppression of ideas, teachers might use an idea from Benson (2003) called the "Grating Paradox." This paradox suggests that people who are intelligent and dynamic often *grate* against each other by virtue of their strong personalities. Dr. Benson suggests that this grating should be encouraged rather than suppressed so that through our differences we can find better, more creative, and useful solutions to most problems. This strategic use of differences has been used successfully in business organizations to foster creatively and productively.

How Can You Get Organizations or People to Change?

If you decide your school needs to change so that you feel more comfortable working there, what can *you* do? Before you take on the role of change agent, you may want to become highly informed about how to work toward change without jeopardizing your career or your health. You *can* promote change, but do not kill yourself in the process. As Ury says in his book *Getting Past No,* if the situation is so unpleasant that you cannot get your needs met, you may need to think of your best alternative plan for working in a particular school or system and put your energies into doing what is best for you. If you feel committed to changing your organization, the following books offer excellent solutions:

◆ *The 7 Habits of Highly Effective People* (Covey, 1989)

The purpose of this extremely popular book is to promote "principle-centered leadership" in order to improve organizations. These are the seven habits:

- Be proactive.
- Begin with the end in mind.
- Put first things first.
- Think win/win. (Interpersonal leadership)
- Seek first to understand, and then to be understood. (Empathetic communication)
- Synergize. (Creative cooperation)
- Sharpen the saw. (Balanced self-renewal)

◆ *Who Moved My Cheese?* (Johnson, 1998)

This book is a parable about how four mice (four aspects of the personality) live in a maze (the place where you look for what you want in life) and live off of cheese (anything and everything we want in life). However, one day the cheese has been moved and the mice show how different parts of our personality deal with change. The moral of the story is that we need to laugh at ourselves, overcome our fears, and look for better things to come to us if we take risks.

◆ *Fish: A Remarkable Way to Boost Morale and Improve Results* (Lundin, Paul, & Christensen, 2000)

Pike's Fish Market in Seattle, Washington, is the model for how organizations can improve by following four easy guidelines:

- Choose your attitude.
- Be present.
- Make someone's day.
- Make your work a fun place to be.

This book offers ideas that appear to be easily implemented by the right kinds of leadership.

♦ *The Tipping Point: How Little Things Can Make a Big Difference* (Gladwell, 2000)

Change does not always happen the way people think it does. According to Gladwell, ideas "tip" (become popular) when certain kinds of people promote those ideas. These people are connectors (people who know lots of people and enjoy getting people of like interests together) and mavens (experts who love to tell other about what they know). Because we have access to so much information, people are relying more often on recommendations from these people rather than the media to decide what to choose. This book can help you understand why certain things work or do not work with children and young people.

♦ *No Excuses: Lesson from 21 High-Performing, High-Poverty Schools* (Carter, 2001)

Carter determines seven common traits of high-performing, high-poverty schools as follows:

• Principals must be free.

• Principals use measurable goals to establish a culture of achievement.

• Master teachers bring out the best in a faculty.

• Rigorous and regular testing leads to continuous student achievement.

• Achievement is the key to discipline.

• Principals work actively with parents to make the home a center for learning.

• Efforts creates ability.

Practice

Changing a behavior is hard to do without practice. Changing your attitudes is a beginning, but it's even more difficult to change your behavior. Here are some suggestions to help you get started.

♦ Use this book to help you reflect on the challenges you face in your school or school district. Give yourself *time* to evaluate your practices based on the BESST Criterion and practice using the five pause-points as you plan your actions.

- Get a copy of *The One-Minute Teacher* by Spencer and Constance Johnson (1986). They show you how to maintain a dialogue with yourself on a regular basis so that you can instill ideas of how you want to be.
- Find a teacher whose attitudes and behaviors you admire. Ask her if you might observe her, talk with her, and get her advice on challenges you are facing.

Change

Your knowledge of the theories and practices presented in this book may influence you to choose to make major changes in your classroom. You may even feel compelled to push for change in your school, district, state, or nation when you think of the obstacles you face. Even if you know what you need to do for your students, you may be working in a system that prevents you from implementing your ideas. In each chapter, I suggest ideas and resources to help you deal with the challenges that have a negative impact on your ability to do your job well. What will you do?

Some school systems have moved far away from the democratic values with which our country was founded. Obsession with testing and accountability has accentuated the need some people have to control others and has even caused people to behave unethically in terms of administering tests and reporting accurate results. How can the system change when most stakeholders are so entrenched in the current trends? As Malcolm Gladwell mentions in *The Tipping Point*, ideas become popular if the right kinds of people promote them. Leadership can come from anywhere and does not have to arise through destructive revolution. The ideas of democracy still exist in the minds and hearts of most citizens. It might take a few well-connected and caring mavens to help schools reach "a tipping point" toward improvement.

Summary

When choosing ways to address the challenges of discipline, unmotivated students, underinvolved or adversarial parents, and tough working conditions, many educators mix and match ideas with sometimes-disastrous effects. Many will jump on the easiest or most attractive bandwagon, picking and choosing from a variety of programs and strategies that often work against each other, and without giving thought as to why these might be good activities. When these choices are unsuccessful, many will blame everyone but themselves for the problems.

Not much has changed since Socrates taught students in the streets of Athens; human nature still leads to abuses of power, but we should yet be able to benefit from having entered the information age. We now have access to information that should help us make better decisions to deal with these age-old challenges. Schools both reflect society and shape it, and for that reason and others, we should do our best to find better ways to run schools.

One could say that both Locke and Hobbes were correct. Mankind is the best in the world and the worst in the world. These two extremes have coexisted in the past, the present, and probably will exist in the future. But we are not debating the nature of mankind. The ideal that shapes our culture is that all men are created equal with inalienable rights. We have rejected the Aristotelian concept that some men are superior to others and therefore have some right to enslave their inferiors or have some kind of power over them. If we believe all men are created equal, why do we continue to base so many of the decisions we make about the students we teach, the parents with whom we confer, and the colleagues with whom we interact on the idea that one person is superior to and should have power over another? Even if you think that adults are superior to children because they are older and deserve to be treated with respect, you certainly would not believe that just because students are young, they do not deserve the respect you would give any human being.

Unfortunately, it seems to be deeply ingrained in our natures that some people must have power over other people, including children. There is a great fear of what would happen if we did not structure most organizations using power-over hierarchy. The concept of equality is damaged by this fear, and thus we continue to *mis*-organize the one place where freedom and equality should be obvious—our schools.

We also have to deal with arrogance. We must find some kind of perspective for the expectations we have for ourselves and for our students. When we set goals, such as *eliminating* learning disparity based on socioeconomic status and race/ethnicity, we set an honorable goal; however, it certainly lets a lot of other people—for example, parents, policy makers, and human service agencies who share the burden that low socioeconomic status and race issues create for children—off the hook. We cannot truly believe that teachers can single-handedly compensate for all of the social factors that contribute to the learning problems for children of poverty. Of course, we can do our best and we can inspire our students to do their best, but we cannot require achievement levels that are so far beyond our reach, that to try for them causes more harm than good.

In many school districts, the concepts of leadership, learning, and organization must undergo a major shift if they want their schools to reflect and sustain the democracy upon which our country was built. An administrator told me recently, "Schools are not democracies." Because of his role at my school, I as a teacher did not feel free to debate with him on this point.

Some of the strategies advocated by researchers and practitioners may not reflect democratic values. For instance, the models that place strict control of classroom discipline and instructional goals in the hands of an authoritarian teacher must be fully evaluated. Even if students appear to need strict control, is this the best way to prepare citizens for a democratic society?

I have provided you with some information that you might use in the systems in which you may have some influence. I hope you will lead from the classroom in order to make your school, your district, and our national system the best places on earth for learning.

References

11 Techniques for Better Classroom Discipline. (n.d.). *Discipline by design: The honor level system.* Retrieved August 29, 2004, from http://www.honorlevel.com/techniques.xml

Argyris, C. (1986). Skilled incompetence. *Harvard Business Review, 64,* 74–79.

Argyris, C. (1991). Teacher smart people how to learn. *Harvard Business Review, 69,* 99–109.

Assertive discipline. (n.d.). Retrieved October 5, 2004, from http://maxweber.hunter.cuny.edu/pub/eres/EDSPC715_MCINTYRE/AssertiveDiscipline.html

Barth, Roland S. (1990). *Improving schools from within.* San Francisco: Jossey-Bass.

Baumrind, D. (1978). Parental disciplinary patterns and social competence in children. *Youth and Society, 9*(3), 239–276.

Baumrind, D. (1991). Parenting styles and adolescent development. In J. Brooks-Gunn, R. Learner, & A. C. Petersen (Eds.), *The encyclopedia on adolescence.* New York: Garland.

Benson, H., & Proctor, W. (2003). *The breakout principle.* New York: Scribner.

Brophy, J. E. (1996). *Teaching problem students.* New York: Guilford.

Brophy, J. E., & McCaslin M. (1992). Teachers' reports of how they perceive and cope with problem students, *Elementary School Journal, 93,* 3–68.

Boeree, G. C. (n.d.). *B. F. Skinner.* Retrieved October 12, 2004, from http://www.ship.euc/~cgboeree/skinner.html

Bond, L., Smith, T., Baker, W., & Hattie, J. (2000, September). *The certification system of the National Board for Professional Teaching Standards: A construct and consequential validity study.* Greensboro: National Board for Professional Teaching Standards, Technical Analysis Group, Center for Educational Research and Evaluation, University of North Carolina-Greensboro.

Carter, S. (2001). *No excuses: Lesson from 21 high-performing, high-poverty schools.* Washington, DC: Heritage Foundation.

Comer, James (1980). *School power: Implementing of an intervention project.* New York: Collier Macmillan.

Connolly, T., Dowd, T., Andrea, C., Nelson, C., & Tobias, L. (1995). *The well-managed classroom: Promoting student success through social skills instruction.* Boys Town, NE: The Boys Town Press.

Cotton, K. (1990). *Schoolwide and classroom discipline.* School Improvement Research Series, Northwest Regional Educational Laboratory. Retrieved August, 29, 2004, from http://www.nwrel.org/scpd/sirs/5/cu9.html

Covaleskie, John F. (1994). Dewey, discipline, and democracy. *Philosophy of Eduction.* Retrieved August 29, 2004, from http://www.ed.uiuc.edu/EPS/PES-Yearbook/94_docs/COVALESK.HTM

Covey, Stephen. (1989). *The 7 Habits of Highly Effective People: Powerful Lessons in Personal Change.* New York: Simon & Schuster.

Creating a climate for learning: Effective classroom management techniques. (n.d.). *Education World.* Retrieved August 29, 2004, from http://www.educationworld.com/a_curr155.shtml

Csikszentmihalyi, M. (1990). *Flow: The psychology of optimal experience.* New York: HarperCollins.

Curwin, R., & Mendler, A. (1999). *Discipline with dignity.* Alexandria, VA: Association of Supervisors and Curriculum Development.

Deci, E. L. (1995). *Why we do what we do: Understanding self-motivation.* New York: Penguin Books.

Dewey, J. (1916). *Democracy and education.* New York: The Free Press.

Dreikurs, R. (1968). *Psychology in the classroom* (2nd ed.). New York: Harper & Row.

Eaker, R., Dufour, R., & Dufour, R. (2002). *Getting started: Reculturing schools to become professional learning communities.* Bloomington, IN: National Education Service.

Educational sponge activities. (n.d.). Retrieved October 10, 2004, from tepserver.ucsd.edu/courses/tep129/EducationalSponges.pdf

Ellis, A. (1975). *A guide to rational living.* North Hollywood, CA: Wilshire Books.

Epstein, J. L., Coates, L., Clark-Salinas, K., Sanders, M. G., & Simon, B. (1997). *Partnership2000 schools manual: Improving school-family community connections.* Baltimore: Johns Hopkins University.

Epstein, J. L. (1989). Building parent-teacher partnerships in inner City schools. *Family Resource Coalition Report, 2, 7.*

Epstein, J. L. (1995). School/family/community partnerships: Caring for the children we share. *Phi Delta Kappan, 76*(9), 701–712.

Evans, R. (2005). Reframing the achievement gap. *Phi Delta Kappan 86*(8), 582–589.

Field, T. (1996). *Bully in sight: How to predict, resist, challenge, and combat workplace bullying.* Wantage, Oxfordshire, UK: Wessex.

Fullan, M., & Hargreaves, A. (1991). *What's worth fighting for in your school?* New York: Teachers College Press.

Galinsky, E. (1988). Parents and teacher-caregivers: Sources of tension, sources of support. *Young Children, 43*(3), 4–12.

Ginsberg, M. (2004). *Motivation matters: A workbook for school change.* San Francisco: Jossey-Bass.

Gladwell, M. (2000). *The tipping point: How little things can make a big difference.* New York: Little, Brown.

Glasser, W. (1986). *Control theory in the classroom.* New York: Harper & Row.

Glasser, W. (1990). *The quality school: Managing students without coercion.* New York: Harper & Row.

Goodlad, J. I. (2004, 1984). *A place called school.* New York: McGraw-Hill.

Henderson, A. T., & Berla, N. (1981). *The evidence grows.* Washington, DC: Center for Law and Education.

Henderson, A. T., & Berla, N. (1995). *A new generation of evidence: The family is critical to student achievement.* Washington, DC: Center for Law and Education.

Henry, M. E. (1996). *Parent-school collaboration: Feminist organizational structures and school leadership.* Albany: State University of New York at Albany. (ERIC Document Reproduction Service No. ED395388)

Jensen, E. (1998). *Teaching with the brain in mind.* Alexandria, VA: Association for Supervision and Curriculum Development.

Johnson, S. (1998). *Who moved my cheese?* New York: Putnam.

Johnson, S., & Johnson, C. (1986). *The one-minute teacher: How to teach others to teach themselves.* New York: William Morrow.

Keyes, Carol R. (n.d.). Parent-teacher partnerships: A theoretical approach for teachers. *Clearinghouse on early education and parenting.* Retrieved October 25, 2004, from http://ceep.crc.uiuc.edu/pubs/katzsym/keyes.html

Keyes, C. (1995). *Creating transitions that support children and families: Beginning the conversation in Westchester.* White Plains, NY: Westchester Education Coalition.

Know when to discipline! (An Education World e-Interview with classroom management expert, Howard Seeman, Ph.D.). (n.d.). Retrieved August 29, 2004, from http://www.education-world.com/a_curr/curr258.shtml.

Kohlberg, L. (1981). *The philosophy of moral development: Moral stages and the idea of justice.* New York: HarperCollins.

Kounin, J. S. (1983). Classrooms: Individual or behavior settings? *Micrographs in teaching and learning* (General Series No. 1). Bloomington, IN: Indiana University, School of Education. (ERIC Document Reproduction Service No. 240070)

Leo, J (1997, June 16). On society. *U.S. News and World Report*, p. 19.

Lortie, D. (1975). *School teacher: A sociological study.* Chicago: University of Chicago Press.

Luce, R. W. (1990). *Motivating the unmotivated.* Retrieved January 22, 2005, from http://honolulu.hawaii.edu/intranet/committees/FacDevCom/guidebk/teachtip/unmotiva.htm

Lundin, S., Paul, H., & Christensen, J. (2000). *Fish: A Remarkable Way to Boost Morale and Improve Results.* New York: Hyperion.

Managing inappropriate behavior in the classroom. (n.d.). Reston, VA: ERIC Clearinghouse on Handicapped and Gifted Children. Retrieved August 29, 2004, from http://www.ericdigests.org/1995-1/behavior.htm

Marchand-Martella, N., Slocum, T., & Martella, R. (2004). *Introduction to direct instruction.* New York: Pearson.

Marshall, M. L. (2001). *Discipline without stress, punishments, or rewards.* Los Alamitos, CA: Piper Press.

Marzano, R. (2003) *What works in schools: Translating research into action.* Alexandria, VA: Association for Supervision and Curriculum Development.

Maslow, A. (1962). *Toward a psychology of being.* New York: Harper.

McEwan, E. K. (1998). *How to deal with parents who are angry, troubled, afraid, or just plain crazy.* Thousand Oaks, CA: Corwin Press.

Meier, D. (1995, 2002). *The power of their ideas.* Boston: Beacon Press.

Mendler, A. N. (1992). *What do I do when…?* Bloomington, IN: National Educational Service.

MetLife. (n.d.). [General news: 2004 and 2003 press releases.] Retrieved December 15, 2004, from http://www.metlife.com

MetLife. (n.d.). *MetLife survey of the American teacher: An examination of school leadership.* [From General news: 2004 and 2003 press releases.] December 15, 2004, from http://www.metlife.com

National Board for Professional Teaching Standards. (n.d.). *Standards and National Board certification.* Retrieved May 9, 2005, from http://www.nbpts.org/standards/index.cfm.

National Board for Professional Teaching Standards. (n.d.). *What teachers should know and be able to do: The five core propositions of the National Board.* Retrieved May 9, 2005, from http://www.nbpts.org/about/coreprops.cfm

National Council for Accreditation of Teacher Educators. (n.d.). *Public standards.* Retrieved May 9, 2005, from http://www.ncate.org/public/standards.asp

National PTA. (2000). *Building successful partnerships: A guide for developing parent and family involvement programs.* Bloomington, IN: National Education Service.

Northey, S. (2005). *Handbook on differentiating instruction in middle and high schools.* Larchmont, NY: Eye On Education.

[Overview.] *Discipline by design: The honor level system.* (n.d.). Retrieved August, 29, 2004, from http://honorlevel.com/x83.xml

Paglin, C. (1999, Spring). Early birds: Kindergartners take their first step to success. *Northwest Education.* [Electronic version at Northwest Regional Educational Laboratory]. Retrieved August 29, 2004, from http://www.nwrel.org/nwedu/spring_99/article3.html

Pauley, J., Bradley, D., & Pauley, J. (2001). *Here's how to reach me: Matching instruction to personality types in your classroom.* Baltimore: Paul H. Brookes.

Payne, R. (1998). *Framework for understanding poverty.* Baytown, TX: RFT.

Powell, D. R. (1989). *Families and early childhood programs.* (Research monographs of the National Association for the Education of Young Children No. 3). Washington DC: National Association for the Education of Young Children. (ERIC Document Reproduction Service No. ED309872)

Reed, R. P., Jones, K., Walker, J. M., & Hoover-Dempsey, K. V. (2000). *Parent's motivation for involvement in children's education: Testing a theoretical model.* Paper presented at the symposium, Parent involvement: The perspectives of multiple stakeholders, at the annual meeting of the American Educational Research Association, New Orleans, LA.

Ryan, K. D., Oestreich, D. K., & Orr, G. A., III. (1996). *The courageous messenger: How to successfully speak up at work.* San Francisco: Jossey-Bass.

Senge, P. (2000). *Schools that learn.* New York: Doubleday.

Sergiovanni, T. J. (1996). *Leadership for the schoolhouse.* San Francisco: Jossey-Bass.

Shank, M. (2005). Common space, common time, common work. *Educational Leadership 62*(8), 16–19.

Sherman, L. (1999, Spring). Educational lessons: Out of the tundra, kids learn to better understand their own and others' Feelings. *Northwest Education.* [Electronic version at Northwest Regional Educational Laboratory]. Retrieved August 29, 2004, from http://www.nwrel.org/nwedu/spring_99/article4.html

Soar, R. S., & Soar, R. M. (1979). Emotional climate and management. In P. L. Perterson & H. J. Walberg (Eds.), *Research on teaching: Concepts, findings, and implications* (pp. 97–119). Berkeley, CA: McCutchan.

Southern Association of Colleges and Schools Council for School Improvement. (n.d.). *Public School Standards.* Retrieved May 9, 2005, from http://www.sacscasi.org/region/standards/SACS_CASI_K-12_Standards_InternetVer.pdf

Sprick, R. S. (1985). *Discipline in the secondary classroom: A problem by problem survival guide.* West Nyack, NY: The Center for Applied Research in Education.

Stolp, S. (1994). *Leadership for school culture.* (Eric Digest 91, June 1994, Clearinghouse on Educational Policy Management). Retrieved January 22, 2005, from http://eric.uoregon.edu/publications/digests/digest091.html

Supovitz, J., & Christman, J. (2005). Small learning communities that actually learn: Lessons for school leaders, *Phi Delta Kappan, 36*(9), 649–651.

Taylor, K. W. (1968). *Parents and children learn together.* New York: Teachers College Press.

Teacher Education Institute. (n.d.). *Teacher effectiveness training.* Retrieved August 29, 2004, from http://www.teachereducation.com/course_outlines/graduate_classroom/tet_outline.htm

Ury, William. (1993). *Getting past no: Negotiating your way from confrontation to cooperation.* New York: Bantam Books. (Original work published 1991.)

U.S. Department of Education. (1997). *Overcoming the barriers to family involvement in Title I schools.* Washington, DC: Author.

What is positive discipline? (n.d.). Retrieved August 29, 2004, from http://www.poistivediscipline.com

What is your classroom management profile? (1996). *Teacher Talk.* Retrieved August 29, 2004, from http://education.indiana.edu/cas/tt/v1i2/what.html

Whitaker, T. (2004). *What great teachers do differently: 14 things that matter most.* Larchmont, NY: Eye On Education.

Whitaker, T., & Fiore, D. J. (2001). *Dealing with difficult parents: And with parents in difficult situations.* Larchmont, NY: Eye On Education.

Wlodkowski, R. J., & Ginsberg, M. B. (1995). *Diversity and motivation: Culturally responsive teaching.* San Francisco: Jossey-Bass.

Wong, Harry. (1991). *The first days of school: How to be an effective teacher.* Sunnyvale, CA: Harry K. Wong.

Wood, K. D. (1994). *Practical strategies for improving instruction.* Columbus, OH: National Middle School Association.

Wubbels, T., & Levy, J. (1993). *Do you know what you look like? Interpersonal relationships in education.* London: The Falmer Press.

Wyatt, J., & Hare, C. (1997). *Work abuse: How to recognize it and survive it.* Rochester, VT: Schenkman Books.

Yerkes, R. M., & Dodson, J. D. (1908). The relation of strength of stimulus to rapidity of habit formation. *Journal of Comparative Neurology and Psychology, 18,* 459–82.

You can handle them all. (n.d.). Retrieved August 29, 2004, from http://www.disciplinehelp.com/teacher/